Praise for *Expressions of the Divine*

"Inga's artwork kindles associations to wonderful memories of the everyday experience. I immediately was drawn to several pieces because of her choices of subject matter which evoked an instant emotional connection for me.

My heart soared when I saw them. Her style of realistic impressionism, full of vivid color and a richness of life, brings a responsiveness that gladdens the heart.

I am thrilled to have several of her pieces hanging in my home. They simply brighten my life."

—Lynn Wiss, Retired Teacher

"Inga and I have been friends for a long time. I have known her through good and bad times. I have watched her painting week after week. We have kept in touch during her physically good and painful days. Through her faith, shown in her words and paintings, there is encouragement and strength for today and tomorrow. I am looking forward for her sharing these words and paintings."

—Van Jones, Retired Minister

Expressions of the Divine

Expressions of the Divine

Ingeborg Martinez

Ingeborg Martinez

All Rights Reserved. No part of this publication may be reproduced in any form or by any means, including scanning, photocopying, or otherwise without prior written permission of the copyright holder.

Copyright Ingeborg Martinez © 2017

ISBN-10: 1-944662-13-8

ISBN-13: 978-1-944662-13-4

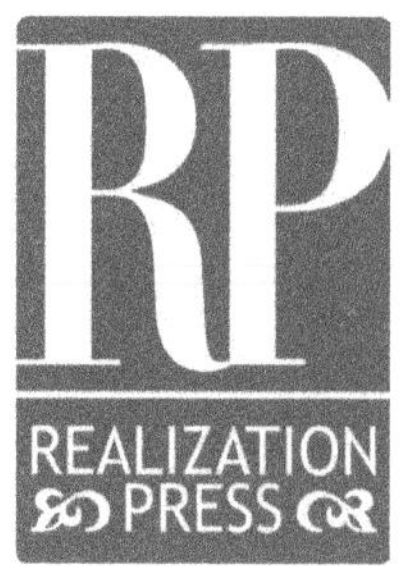

Realization Press Publication Date: March 2017

Cover Art by Ingeborg Martinez

Contents

CHAPTER 2   DIVINE TRUTH

CHAPTER 3   HUMAN EMOTIONS

CHAPTER 4   HEALING, HARMONY AND BALANCE

CHAPTER 5   DIVINE GUIDANCE

Foreword by Diana Henderson

Art always has a message. In the hands of an artist, a paintbrush has the power to inflame the senses, evoke a visceral response, affect the mood, captivate the imagination or uplift the consciousness. My favorite artists have always been those who are touched by Spirit, who seek to transport us into a realm of beauty and love. In my view, these gifted souls are messengers of light. I consider Ingeborg (Inga) Martinez one such artist.

Inga has taken her work a step beyond what lies upon the canvas, however. She was guided to give voice to the messages behind the visual images and to share the heart song of the universe through poetry as well as pictures. Spirit speaks through her words and paintings to reveal a greater canvas. As she expresses beautifully in "The Embroidery of Life," only the Divine can see the complete, finished masterpiece, but by combining her art with inspiring words from Spirit, she gives us a glimpse into the grand design.

In this book, Inga invites us to see the world through Divine eyes and recognize that even the mundane and sensory aspects of life are part of that tapestry. When we walk through human existence in the knowing that the Divine experiences every nuance of life with us, we begin to savor each moment and rise into a higher perspective.

Inga understands this on a deep level. She has the capacity to perceive the light in everyone, to behold the Creator in all things.

Ingeborg Martinez

Sorrow and pain are not foreign to any artist. Like most, Inga feels deeply and bravely imparts the way forward through those emotions of grief and fear that we all know so well.

When I first encountered this book, I was having a difficult day. Nothing Earth-shattering was happening—just a night of insomnia followed by a series of minor challenges. Nonetheless, after reading a few of the entries and embracing the energy of the art, I realized that I needed those words and images in my life at that exact moment. They felt like a gift from the Divine sent directly to my heart. Tears came to my eyes more than once as I absorbed the truths on these pages. While the concepts were certainly not new to me and in many cases articulated beliefs I already held dear, they were expressed in a unique way—through the union of paintings and verse—and evoked in my consciousness a definite shift toward inner peace.

I invite readers to pick up this book on those days when life is less than ideal and peruse its pages until you come upon the message meant for you in that moment. Once there, let your consciousness flow into the painting; allow the words and the works of art to find a home in your psyche until you feel your true self again. Those who are troubled will find shelter here. In times when the sun shines through your soul and illumines every aspect of your life, you will discover a kindred voice in these pages as well. All you need to do in such cases is allow the spirit within to guide you to the message that strengthens your knowing and honors your light.

~ Diana Henderson, founder of the Order of Archangel Michael and Sacred Heart Soul Healing, ascension artist and author of *Grandfather Poplar* and *Kindred of the Crystal Kingdom*

Dedication

**This book is dedicated to
Joshua**

Ingeborg Martinez

Acknowledgements

Without the loving, patient and helpful support of so many beautiful souls during my lifetime, this book would not have been possible. My heartfelt *thank you* to all who helped to enlighten my path:

Marty, my ex-husband, who gifted the first oil paints and supported my spiritual search.

Dominic, my sweet son, who contributed to many paintings, inspired by photos taken during his bicycle races.

My gorgeous daughter, Veronica, who loves my paintings and later wants to preserve as many as possible. She also acted patiently as model for a number of charcoal drawings.

My beloved toy poodle Snowball, most loyal soul, day and night at my side patiently waiting until Mommy is finally finished working.

Joshua, my dearest and beloved friend, who tirelessly, patiently and most lovingly encouraged me to publish this book.

Don Mason, who invited me with open arms into the Open Studio at the Pullen Arts Center in Raleigh so many years ago.

My dear artist friends at the Open Studio: Van, Dan, JoAnn, Joan, Sondra, Bucky, Doreen, Dolores, Adele and all the others.

All the wonderful people at Pullen and Sertoma Park in Raleigh, North Carolina, who make the art centers such a comfortable place to be.

The Women's Club of Raleigh who embraced me lovingly as a member. They kindly made me not once but twice *Artist of the Month* and exhibited many of my paintings. I was also able to participate at the yearly Arts Festivals and was honored with several prizes.

The doctors and staff at Internal Medicine and Pediatrics in Cary, North Carolina, especially Mrs. Ersilia Sarno, who not only took exceptional care of my physical health, but also exhibited many of my paintings a couple of times in the practice.

Drew Becker, who agreed to publish this book.

Diana Henderson who initiated me into The Order of Achangel Michael and selflessly created the Foreword to my book.

Charles Register, who photographed my paintings with dedication and professionality.

Mary Anne Jenkins, professional artist and teacher, who taught me the art of *impressionism.*

Larry Dean, professional artist, teacher and musician, who lovingly guides me through each painting.

Ingeborg Martinez

Shelley Kraft, my longtime counselor, who helped me with great dedication and love through many ups and downs in my life.

Veronica Vela, energy healer, minister, Reiki master and spiritualist, who guided me through many health and personal challenges.

Sherrie Dillard, a most gifted psychic, who confirmed that this book would one day be published.

Kevin P. Hopper, Attorney, who devotedly and diligently guided me successfully through the maze of a divorce

My spirit guide and guardian angel. Without their constant guidance and nudging, I would be too timid to offer my art and spiritual messages in a book.

Thank you again and God bless you all!

Introduction

To quote Mother Teresa: "I am the pencil and God is the hand."

Please regard this book, which has been guided by the spirit world, as an inspiration for readers to connect with their spirit, to meditate and contemplate and to find peace and harmony by reading the texts and looking at the paintings.

Most of all, I hope this book will be a blessing to everybody, lifting all of us higher into the realms of the divine.

Enjoy the journey through my book as a tool to just *DO NOTHING!* Read the texts that came through from the spirit world; contemplate them or not; either is perfect! There is absolutely no need to understand. Your spirit already understands. It will come to your human mind in its own time.

This book taught me that I am NOT alone! There are so many helpful and willing souls along the path to share the love of God. It is not about *being perfect* but just *being*. My intention is to express myself and hopefully inspire, encourage and uplift my readers. The paintings and texts were made manifest from my heart to convey love, peace, harmony, joy and well-being. Almost every painting has some kind of personal story behind it. Most of the art was created from photos taken while *living my life*. The individual stories are included as notes at the end of each chapter.

Ingeborg Martinez

For a better understanding of how my life has evolved so far, here are some highlights for you:

My life began in Stuttgart, Germany, where I was born in 1955 and raised by a *blue-collar family* in the town of Gerlingen, a suburban town of Stuttgart. I was very blessed to have been surrounded by a large extended family. My father's side of the family immigrated in the 1800s to Hungary. After WWII they had to depart from Hungary leaving everything behind. His family went back to the same area where my ancestors had come from, the south of Germany. Most of them settled in Gerlingen.

My mother's family had a similar experience. Her ancestors moved to Poland about 200 years earlier and settled in and around the town of Krakau. After WWII they also had to leave and moved to Esslingen in southern Germany.

Growing up, I unfortunately still experienced the aftermath of this era. My father and mother were *children* and *victims* of this war. My father became a German soldier at the age of 15 and my mother was abducted by Russians to Siberia at the age of 14 where she was treated as a prisoner of war. After both had been POWs for many years, they came home in 1952 with wounds on all levels.

Traditionally, I was raised as a Roman Catholic, primarily through Catholic classes held at school and attended masses at church with my grandmother, Hermine. In my teenage years, I abandoned the church. I did not agree with most of the doctrines and teachings.

Instead, I wanted to concentrate on school and make a career for myself.

Two months before my fifteenth birthday, I had the opportunity to be employed by Daimler-Benz in Stuttgart, Germany. There I started my career with an entry level job as an office assistant. At the same time, I attended business school and graduated in 1973 as *office clerk with stenography*. To continue my education, I went to a private night school and graduated in 1974 with a diploma as an *executive secretary* . The reward for my education was an interesting position as an executive secretary dealing with Daimler-Benz companies all over the world.

After being a secretary over twelve years, I wanted to improve myself. In 1987 I again started night school. Two years later, in 1989, I graduated with a degree in business. This allowed me to move up to a demanding position in the Controlling and Budgeting Department for trucks.

I was married to my first husband in 1979. Unfortunately, several years later, we were divorced without children.

In 1989 I married my second husband, an American citizen. The marriage was blessed with two children whom we adopted from Romania. The adventures I experienced through these two adoptions would fill a book on their own! Both children are now adults living their own fulfilled lives.

The second phase of my extraordinary journey began in December 1998 when I came to the USA with my family. After spending 22 years in Germany, my husband was homesick and wanted to *come home*. Luckily, he was transferred through his company to Raleigh, North Carolina. Experiencing America for the first time, I went through quite a strong cultural shock. In my naivete, I truly believed the USA would be like Germany.

The adjustment took a while but, nonetheless, I immediately fell in love with the country, the wonderful people, the impressive towns and breathtaking nature. Traveling up and down the East Coast in the first years was a complete delight.

Ingeborg Martinez

Did I mention that I barely spoke the language arriving here? Yes, blank-eyed I listened to all the conversations and tried to stumble out some words. Here again, the kindness and helpfulness of people guided me through rough communication waters.

Hands-on practice in the American world, attending Lifelong Education at the North Carolina State University, and reading mountains of books supported me in becoming more fluent and knowledgeable in this wonderful language. Today, only my accent still gives me away as coming from Germany; otherwise nobody would notice anymore. Thrillingly, in November 2003, I officially was pronounced an *American Citizen* and I have become as American as can be!

The second marriage broke up unexpectedly after being wedded for 27 years, leaving me with my toy-poodle, Snowball, whom I love dearly. He is the ripe age of 14 years, survived anal gland cancer, a severe knee injury, and suffers from several age-related ailments. He is the sweetest, most loving little guy and it is an honor to take care of him.

On the spiritual front: After I had two children, I wanted them to be introduced to the Catholic faith like I was as a child. I went back to church and rekindled my former religious education. By this time, I was so intrigued that I started to explore the spiritual side of life more and more which led me to study not only the Bible, but also brought me into contact with *new age teachings*: metaphysics, mediumship, psychic phenomena, etc. Slowly, I evolved my own spirituality which guided me to receive texts written down with my left hand. In my search, I also was introduced to the universal healing energy Reiki. I have completed level one, two and the first level of the Reiki Master training.

Experiencing difficult circumstances in my family life and being challenged by several health issues— including four back surgeries, a hysterectomy, a rotator cuff surgery and being in constant pain from fibromyalgia—I needed to explore the spiritual world looking for answers and used the painting to express my inner view of the world.

My passion for painting started very innocently around 1994 in Germany after my husband presented me with a beautiful wooden box full of oil color and some brushes as a birthday gift. Soon afterwards I was sitting down with my children at the table. They were drawing and I was painting. Together we had so much fun. Because of time issues (working mother), I could not paint too much in the beginning. When I came to the United States, I decided to be a stay-at-home mother and had more time on my hand.

Going through the *Leisure Ledger* of the town of Raleigh, where I lived, I came across a course called *Open Studio* held by Don Mason. What a delightful teacher he was and in a short time we became friends. He gave me my first instructions about how to paint in oil, the use of composition, the mixing of color, etc. Unfortunately, Don Mason passed away in April 2009 and I still miss him dearly. All the people who attended the *Open Studio* were the sweetest persons and going to painting Monday mornings became one of the highlights of my week. A couple years later, I started to take additional advanced courses with Mary-Ann Jenkins to study the painting technique *impressionism*. After Mary-Ann retired, I continued to study with Leslie Pruneau until my health started to decline and I had to take a hiatus from painting at Pullen Park.

I painted from my home without instruction, adjusting to the health issues. During that time, I had to endure three surgeries, many doctor visits and tests. The surgeries helped to restore my back and shoulder problems. Unfortunately, the diagnosed Fibromyalgia is chronic. Here too I have to adjust painting around the state of my health.

Ingeborg Martinez

Over the years, I have created more than one hundred paintings and was fortunate to exhibit them in several places in Cary and Raleigh. For example, in October 2015 and February 2017, I was *The Artist of the Month* at the Woman's Club in Raleigh and showed many of my paintings.

I am back at the Open Studio at Pullen Park and advanced painting with Larry Dean at the Sertoma Park, both in Raleigh. Additionally, I also paint at home.

I hope that this introduction gives you a short overview of my life and who I am, and this book will help you to find peace, joy, harmony and the love of God while reading the pages and looking at the paintings.

God bless you!

Chapter 1

Creator and Creations

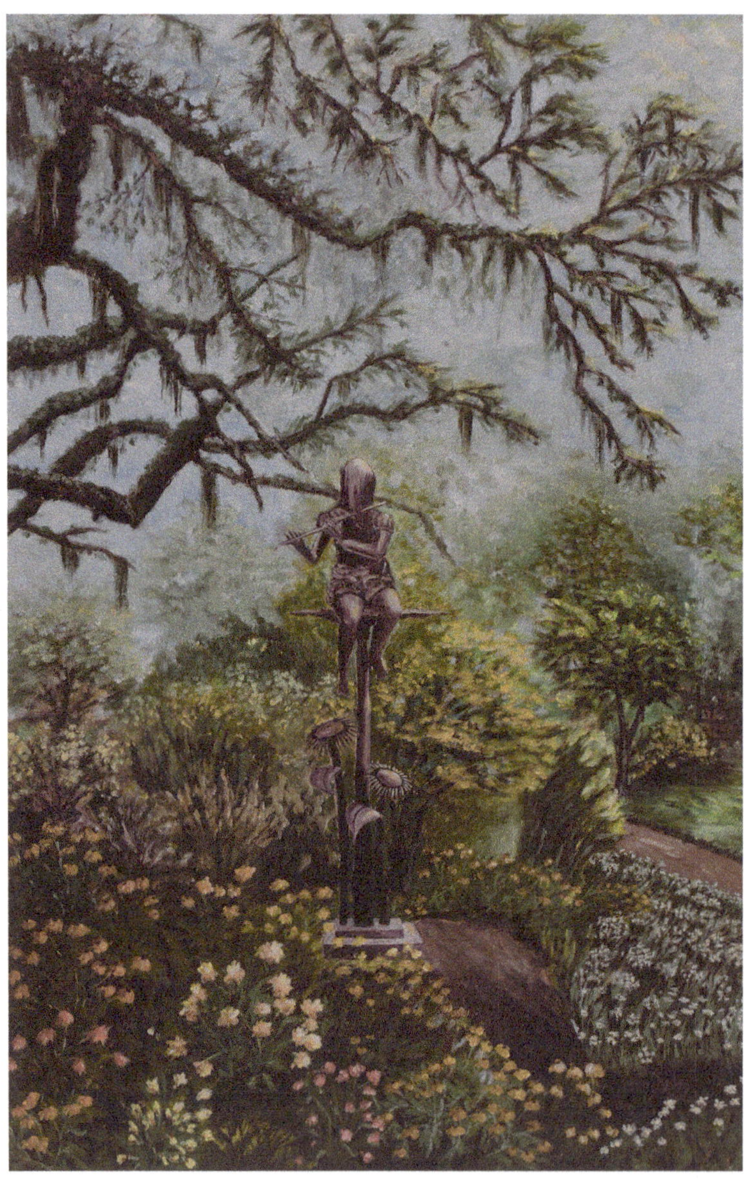

LIGHT AND LIFE

Greetings from the Divine

Dearly beloved child,

How I marvel being in your presence!
Words are not able to describe the Love I have for you!

My brave, brave soldier walking the treacherous paths for me on earth.
How I adore you, my child!
Be granted all the protection you need day and night.
I ask you to proudly and firmly
hold your sword of truth and light up high.
All negative energies will dissipate around you so that you may be a
shining beacon of love and truth for all around you.

None of your tasks are menial.
None of your words are without power.
Your presence in itself is of utmost importance!

Let Me be your guiding light on this marvelous day, and there will be
only joy and merry in the wake.
Thoroughly, I so love working with you!
Be eternally blessed, my beloved child.

In devotion

Ingeborg Martinez

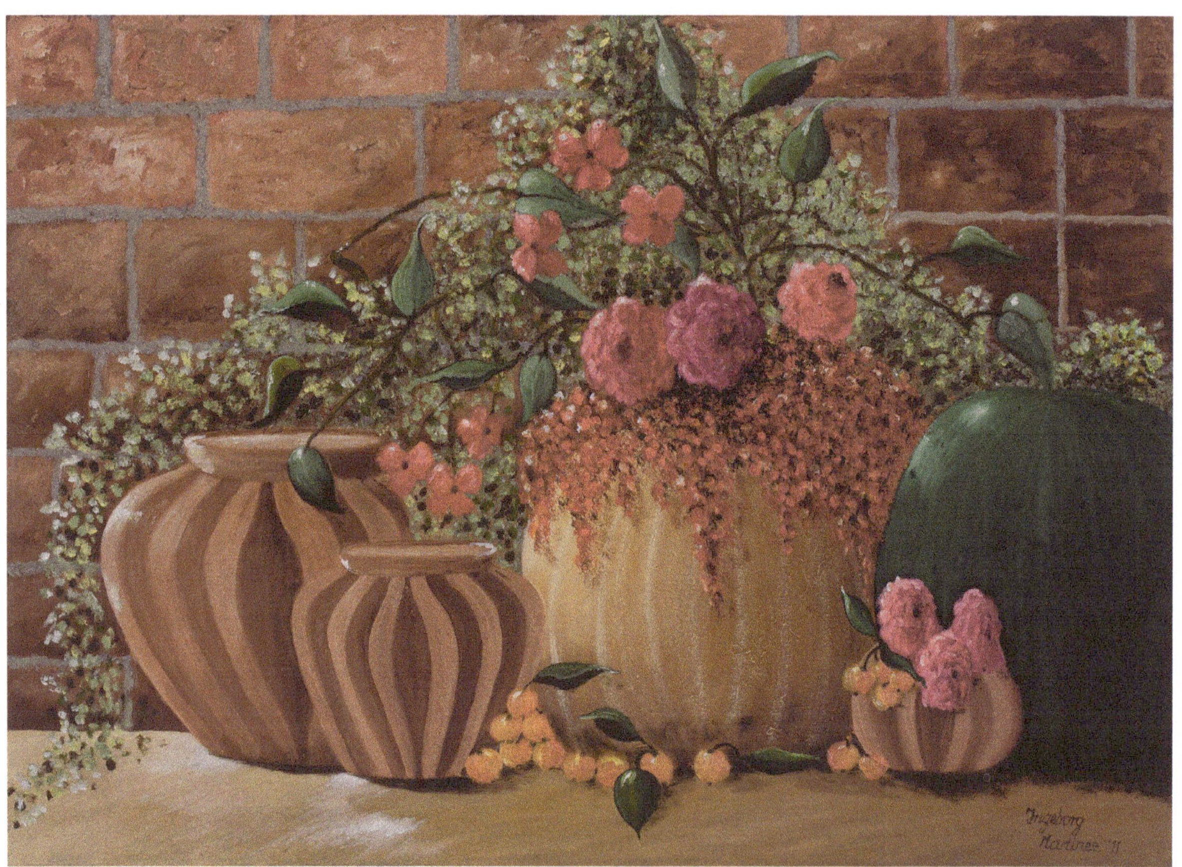

The Embroidery of Life

Everybody has his own goal in life.
To keep your own inner peace,
refrain from judging these goals.

Every single soul on this beautiful earth has its
own and personal life path.

Imagine an embroidery in the working:
Usually you start in the middle and work your way outward.
There are so many different colors of strings to use,
so many different kinds of little forms and shapes to embroider.
First it looks chaotic and makes no sense.
But, oh so slowly, real images start to appear:

There, it is a flower!
And here, it is a vase!
Finally, the piece is finished:
A Masterpiece!

Each soul brings its individual *color* to the whole.
Each little form or shape is a soul group,
working diligently together for the whole.
Together they form *The Masterpiece!*

So, don't judge because you are not able
to see the finished Masterpiece that God has created.

This is how you achieve real inner peace!

Ingeborg Martinez

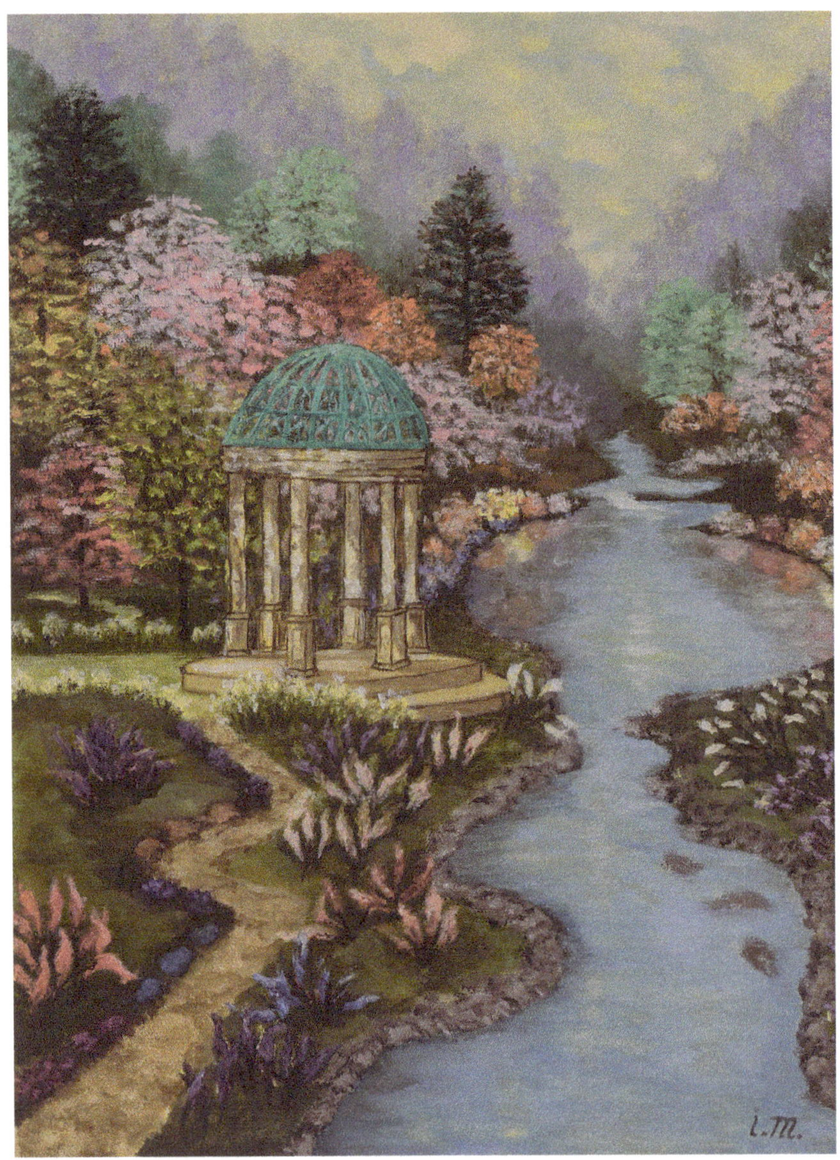

The Light of My Heart

You are the light of My Heart!
There is nothing but LOVE for you.
Look closely and you will see ME,
your Creator,
all around you.

Let ME fill your heart today
with my never-ending love,
and experience the miracle
that you truly are!

Ingeborg Martinez

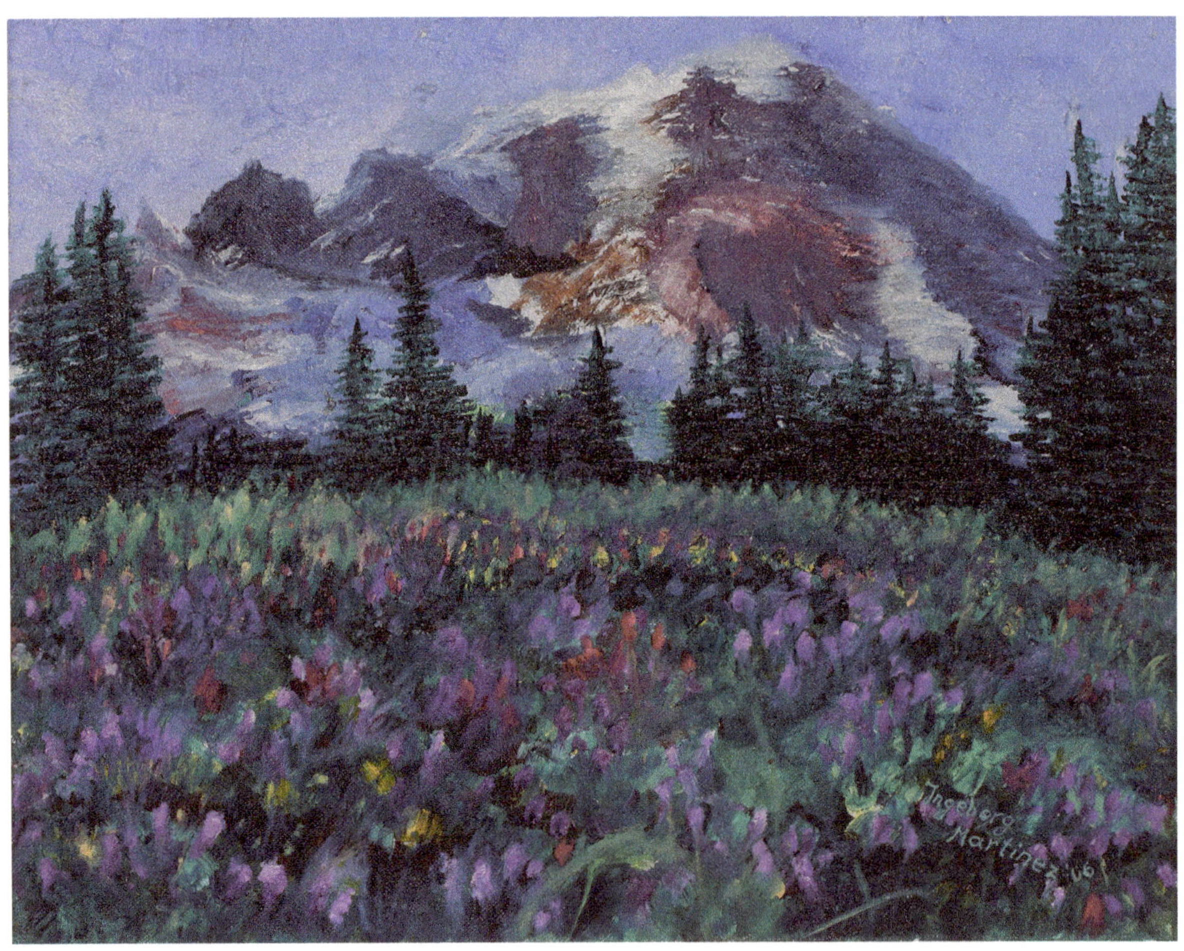

Your Creations

Bring your whole being into everything you do.
Connect consciously with everything and
everyone around you.

Recognize and look at your creations.
You are a marvelous creator
created in the same image as your main source.

Give thanks to everything in and around you!
Be happy for your creations.
Smile at them and they will smile back at you,
returning your gratitude to the fullest!

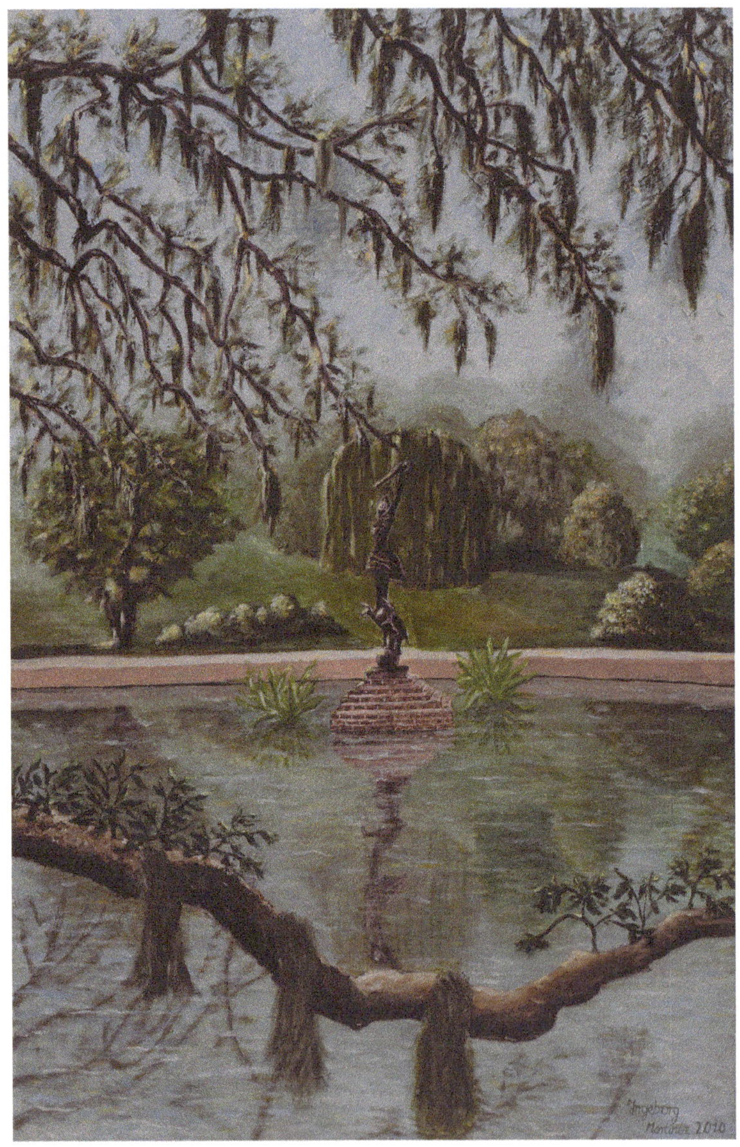

Your True Being

Your life is precious to ME;
I hold you in the highest regard!

Light and Glory is your true being and
nothing is able to hide it.

In the time of your earthly endeavor,
you think your light can be lost,
which is only a mistake.

Your light truly shines eternally,
a bright star in a sparkling universe
full of love.

Ingeborg Martinez

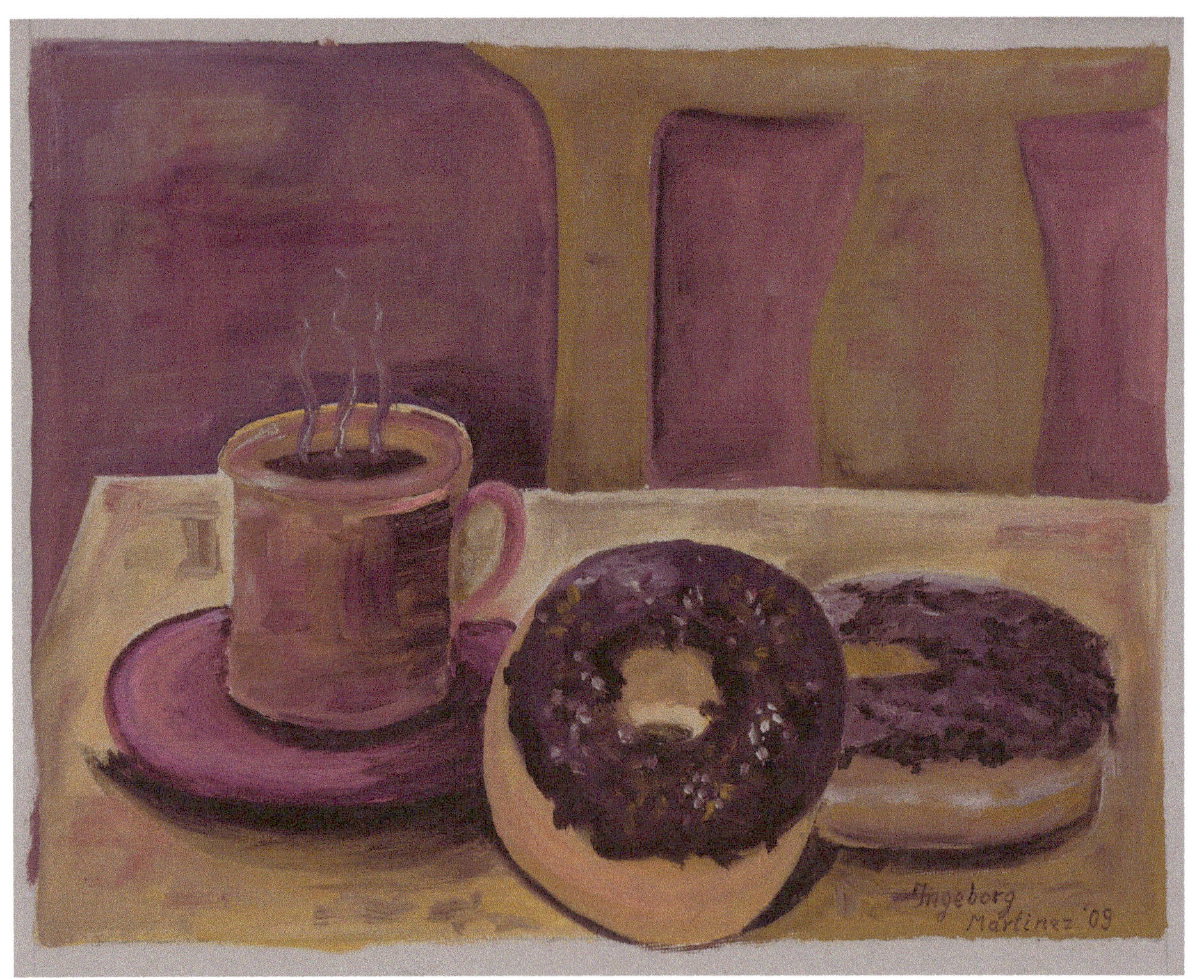

ETERNITY AND TIME

NOW is the Only Time that Exists

NOW is the only time that exists.
For you with your human mindset,
this is very difficult to understand.

Trust Me always, Your Creator.
I am here with you, right NOW!

Open your ears and
listen to the sweet sounds of nature.
Open your eyes and
see the beauty of GOD that surrounds you.
Experience the exclusive smells of life which
include food, flowers, your fellow humans
and so much more.

I Am in the Here and NOW.
Savor it, be uplifted, energized and
filled with my LOVE for you.

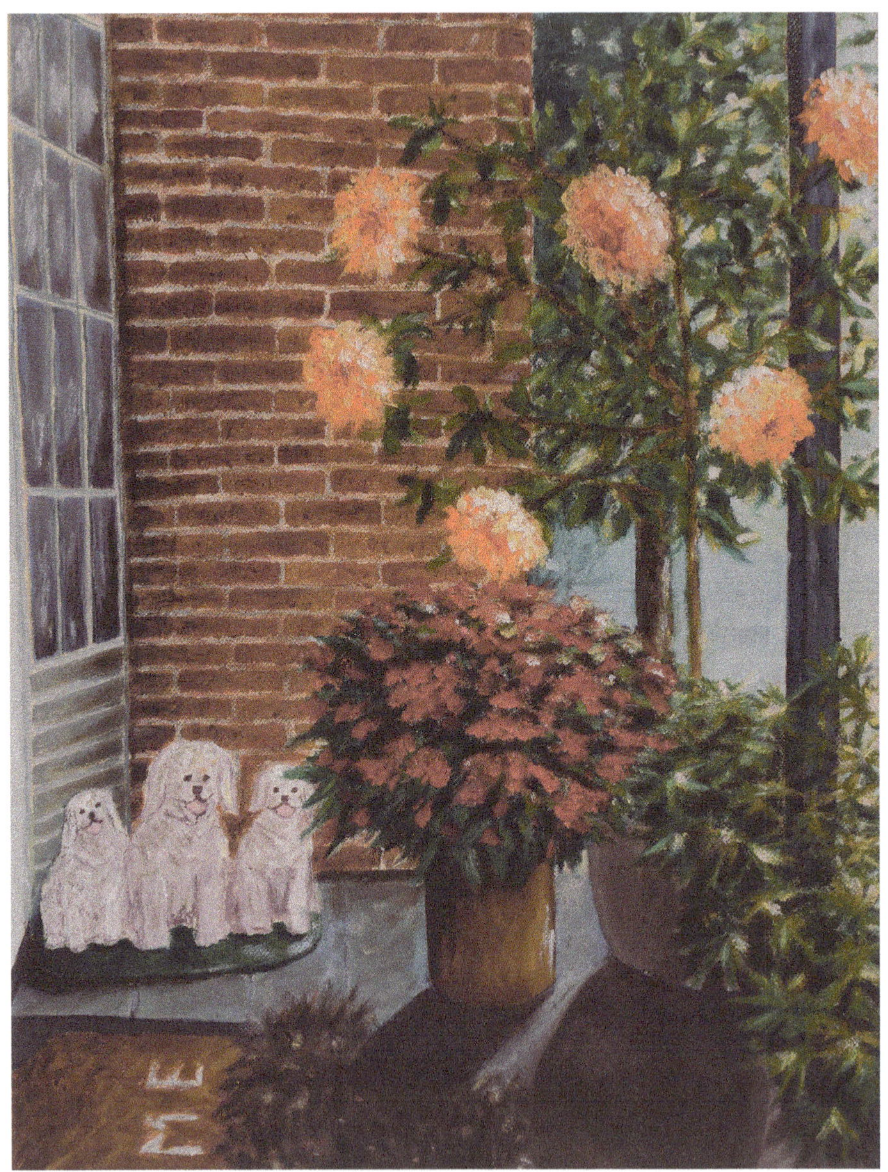

Reality

Yesterday is only a dream.

How do you feel waking up from
a dream in the night?

First, you are confused and
then you realize it was only a dream!

Today is today and
only today exists.

Shake the dream from your shoulders and
fully enjoy today!

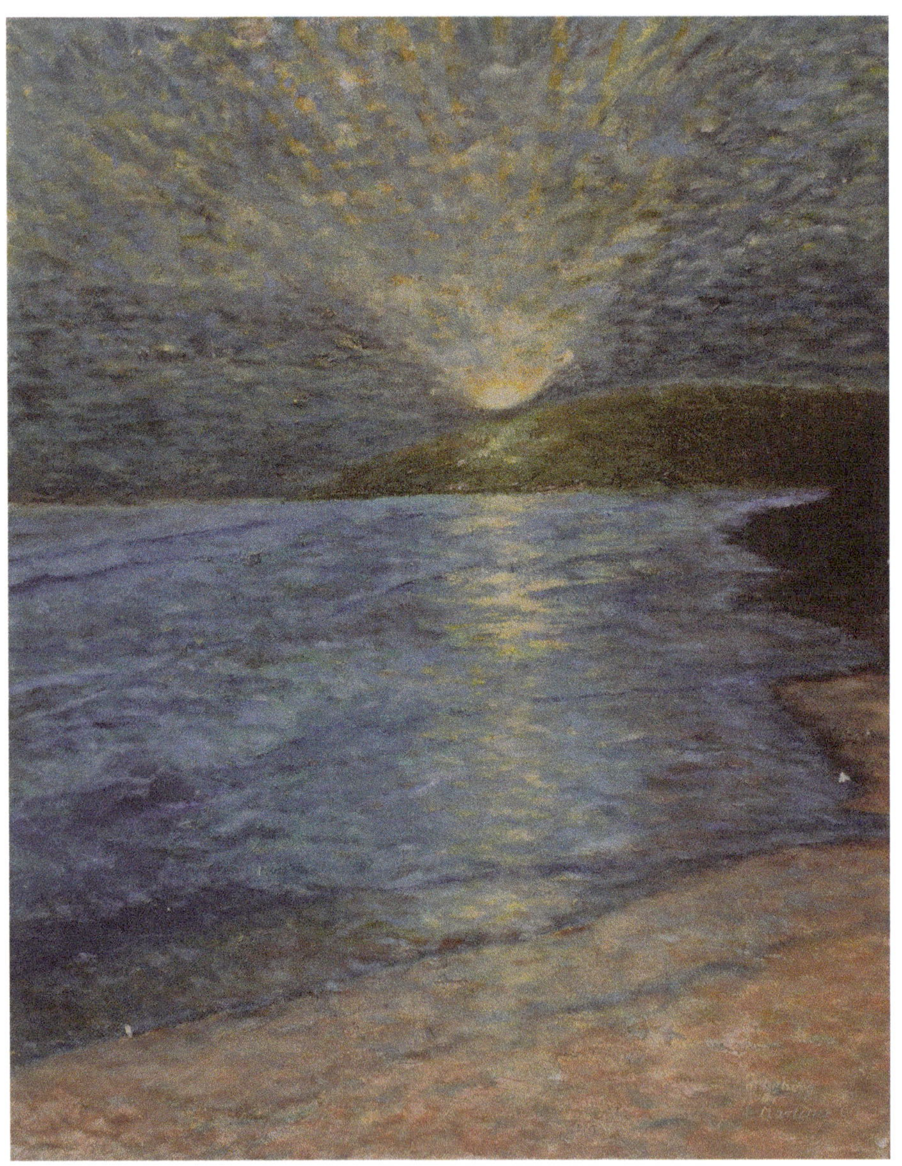

Everything and Nothing

Today I am talking to you about *Nothing*.
Do you understand the concept of Nothing?
No, you don't.

Let me explain to you the concept of Nothingness:
Nothing is Everything and Everything is Nothing.
Black is white and white is black.
All is One and the One is ME.
Always, forever, unchanging, solid substance.
I am in you and you are in ME.

You are safe in ME.
You are forever in ME.
You are Me and I am you.
You still don't understand,
but this is the *Truth!*

Ingeborg Martinez

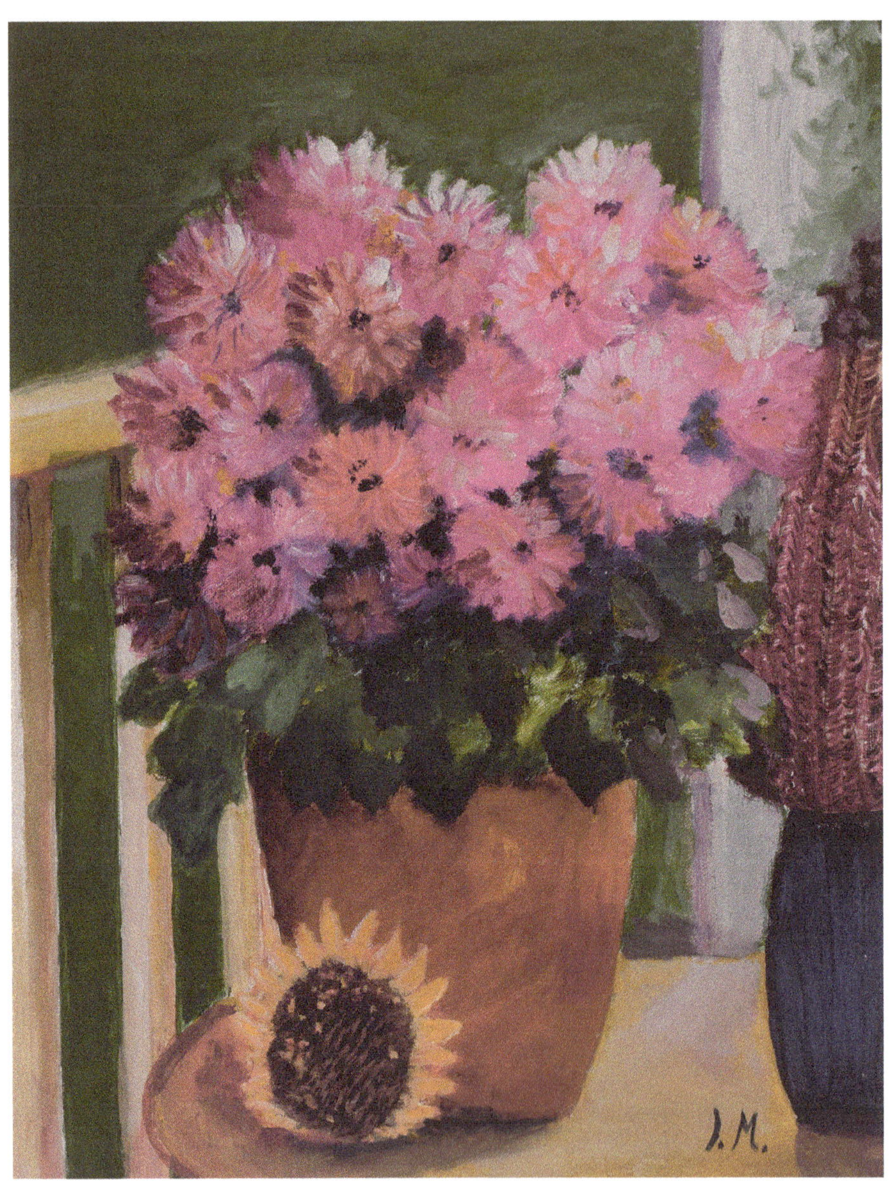

DUALITY

Love and Ego

Everything you see is man-made.
The Truth is found in the Love you project into it.
Love often is defused because it is tainted by your ego.

Listen to the Truth in yourself.
Everything that makes you ONE with ME
is the *real result!*

Ingeborg Martinez

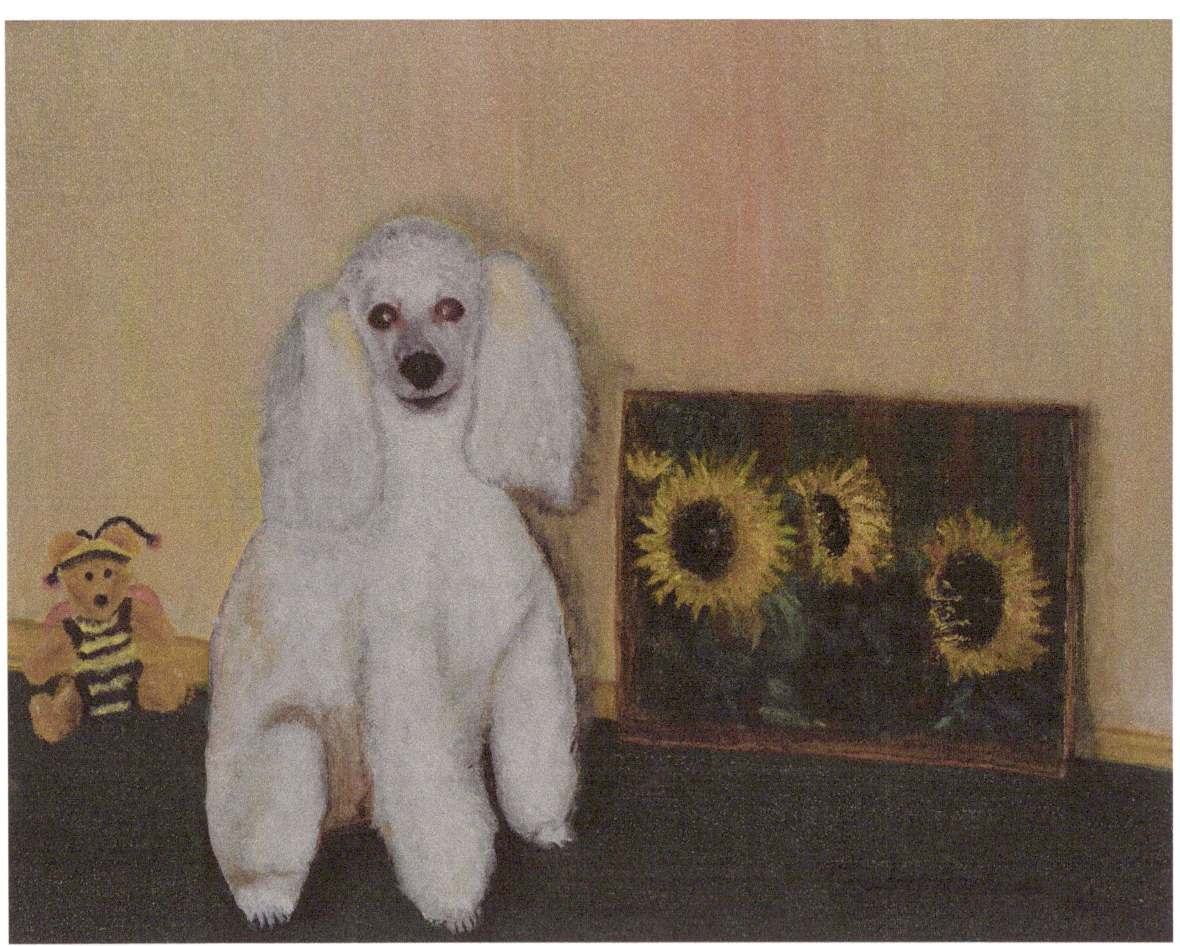

SOUL AND BODY

A Poem for Snowball

Gentle soul in a gentle body.
So much love is given to you.

Gentle soul in a gentle body.
So much love comes out of you.

My heart is joyful just thinking of you.
My soul is grateful for being with you.

Gentle soul, you have blessed my life.
Gentle body, you have graced in style.

You are the best that ever happened to me.
You are my comfort in life against stings of the bee.

Notes

Light and Life

The Flute Player on page 2
Text: "Greetings from the Divine"
Oil on canvas, 24" x 36" – 2010
Subject: Brookgreen Gardens, SC
During a vacation in Pawley's Island, South Carolina, we made a visit to the Brookgreen Gardens. I took many breathtaking photos there which resulted in several paintings. *The Flute Player* is one of my favorite paintings.

Pumpkin and Roses on page 4
Text: "Embroidery of Life"
Oil on canvas, 28" x 20" – 2012
Subject: Fruit and flowers
With this creation I wanted to show the joy of summer in the combination of pumpkins, melons and flowers.

Solitude on page 6
Text: "Light of my Heart"
Oil on canvas, 12" x 16" – 2014
Subject: Gazebo in a fantasy landscape
While wandering through a beautiful landscape that looks like it comes out of a fairy tale, the gazebo is an invitation to rest and be in the shade. Here I let my fantasy create the most vibrant colors coming directly out of the heart.

Purple Meadow on page 8
Text: "Your Creations"
Oil on canvas, 18" x 14" – 2006
Subject: Landscape
This painting is among my first attempts to apply the *impressionism* technique. I learned to use perspective and mixing of color.

Diana on page 10
Text: "Your True Being"
Oil on canvas, 24" x 36" - 2010
Subject: Sculptor at Brookgreen Gardens, South Carolina
Diana is one of several paintings that I created after visiting Brookgreen Gardens in South Carolina. She depicts the goddess of hunting, located in the middle of a small pond surrounded by greenery, flowers, and the most beautiful oak trees hanging with moss.

Ingeborg Martinez

Eternity and Time

Threesome on page 12
Text: "NOW is the Only Time that Exists"
Oil on canvas, 14" x 11" – 2009
Subject: Cup and donuts
Many people are fond of donuts and we like to have our coffee with them. Under the
instruction of Leslie Pruneau, I decided to bring a cup and two donuts to painting class and
create the assembly in my own way of seeing. I hope you enjoy not only the painting but also a
real donut with coffee or tea!

Welcome on page 14
Text: "Reality"
Oil on canvas, 14" x 18" – 2009
Subject: Entrance to our apartment
The hibiscus on the right side was an extremely loyal companion for many years. Here, I
painted it when it was around two years old. I was so fortunate to enjoy it for six more years.
The group of white dogs is still in my possession and these three beauties are now protecting
my new entrance. I took a photo while I was living in the Huntington Apartments in
Morrisville, North Carolina.
It looked so inviting and made a great subject for a painting.

Impression of Sundown on page 16
Text: "Everything and Nothing"
Oil on canvas, 16" x 20" – 2007
Subject: Beach in Montenegro, former Yugoslavia
In 2007, Mary-Anne Jenkins asked her students in her painting class to paint an impressionistic
image either from imagination or from a black and white photo. I decided to paint my image
from an old photo taken on the beach in Montenegro in 1987 at sundown.

Duality

Mums and Sunflower on page 18
Text: "Love and Ego"
Oil on canvas, 14" x 18" – 2000
Under the instruction of Don Mason, I painted this image as one of my earlier paintings in the Open Studio at Pullen Park. Working on it he taught me composition, perspective and the setting of shades.

Soul and Body

Snowball with Bee Bear page 20
Text: "A Poem for Snowball"
Oil on canvas, 14" x 11" – 2005
Subject: My toy poodle Snowball
One day, coming home from the studio where I was painting the sunflowers, I put the painting on the floor and said "Hello" to Snowball. He was sitting so sweetly next to the painting, being happy that his Mommy was home, I had to take a photo. This photo in turn inspired me to paint him and is my first painting of him. More were following.

Chapter 2

Divine Truth

God's Love

    I Love you forever

    A Love Letter from God

    True Love

God's Presence

    My Presence

    I Am

    Your True Source

God and Friend

    God is your Friend

    God's Mercy

    Mercy

    Desire for God

    Be near to Me

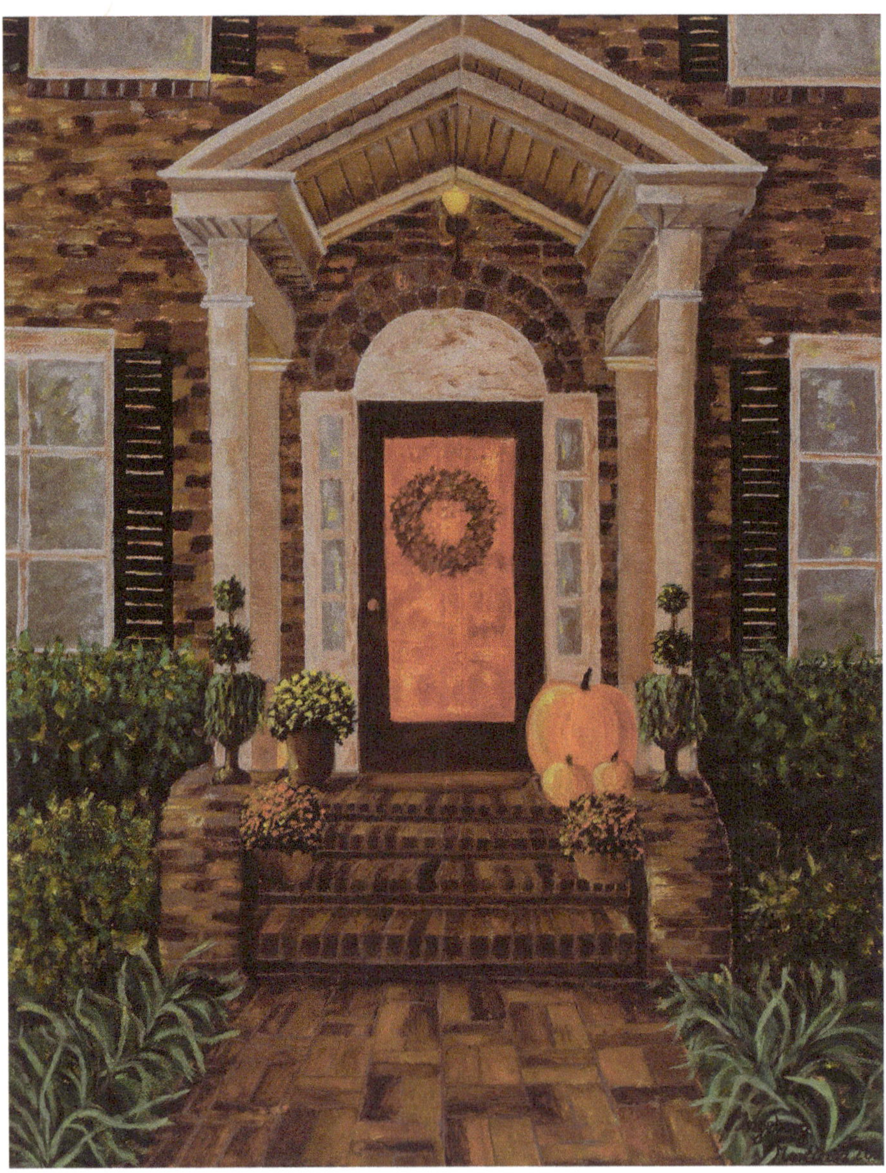

I Love You Forever

Finally, here you are:
Welcome back into My Holy Presence!

You had a rough road to travel.
Pain and suffering were your companions.

You are so weak and exhausted, overwhelmed with your daily tasks.

Though you daily prayed to ME!
Sometimes not even knowing.

You have arrived:
You are here again in quiet and stillness.

Finally, I can tell you:
I love you;
I love you;
I love you forever!

Ingeborg Martinez

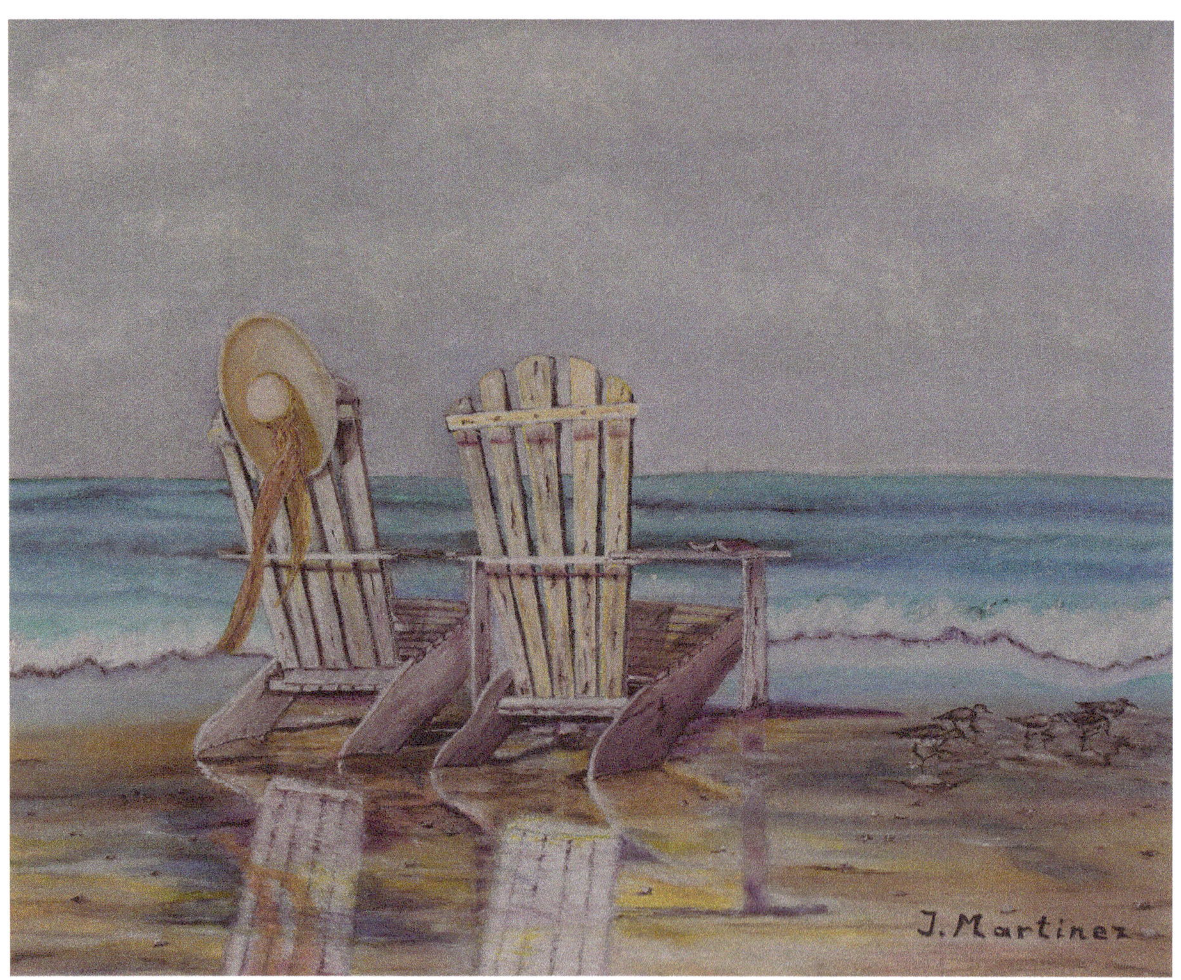

A Love Letter from GOD

You are my precious child forever!

My love for you is deeper than the deepest ocean;
Higher than the highest mountain;
Sweeter than the sweetest wedding and
lasts as long as eternity!

It lasts forever!

I am here with you right now,
caressing you in my presence,
singing into your ear the sweetest love song,
created only for you.

Be still and hear My angels singing tribute to you!

Ingeborg Martinez

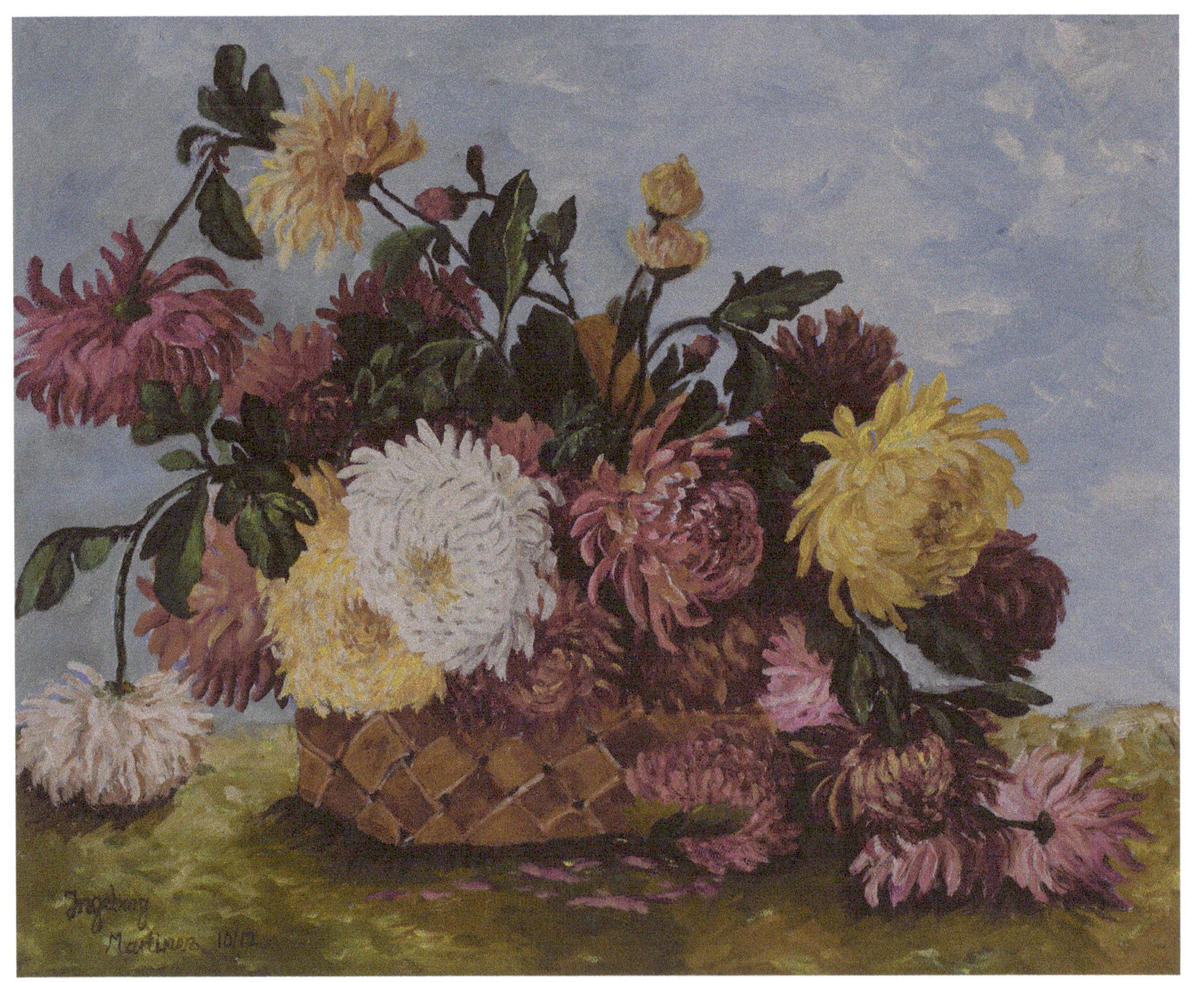

True Love

Love on earth is a fickle thing.
Not always do you get what you want.

Yet, there is truth in
every person, thing or circumstance.

Love resides in you as your true inheritance.

Love yourself dearly!
Stop to judge yourself and see yourself
in a kind and tender light.

Do this and love for all will follow!

Ingeborg Martinez

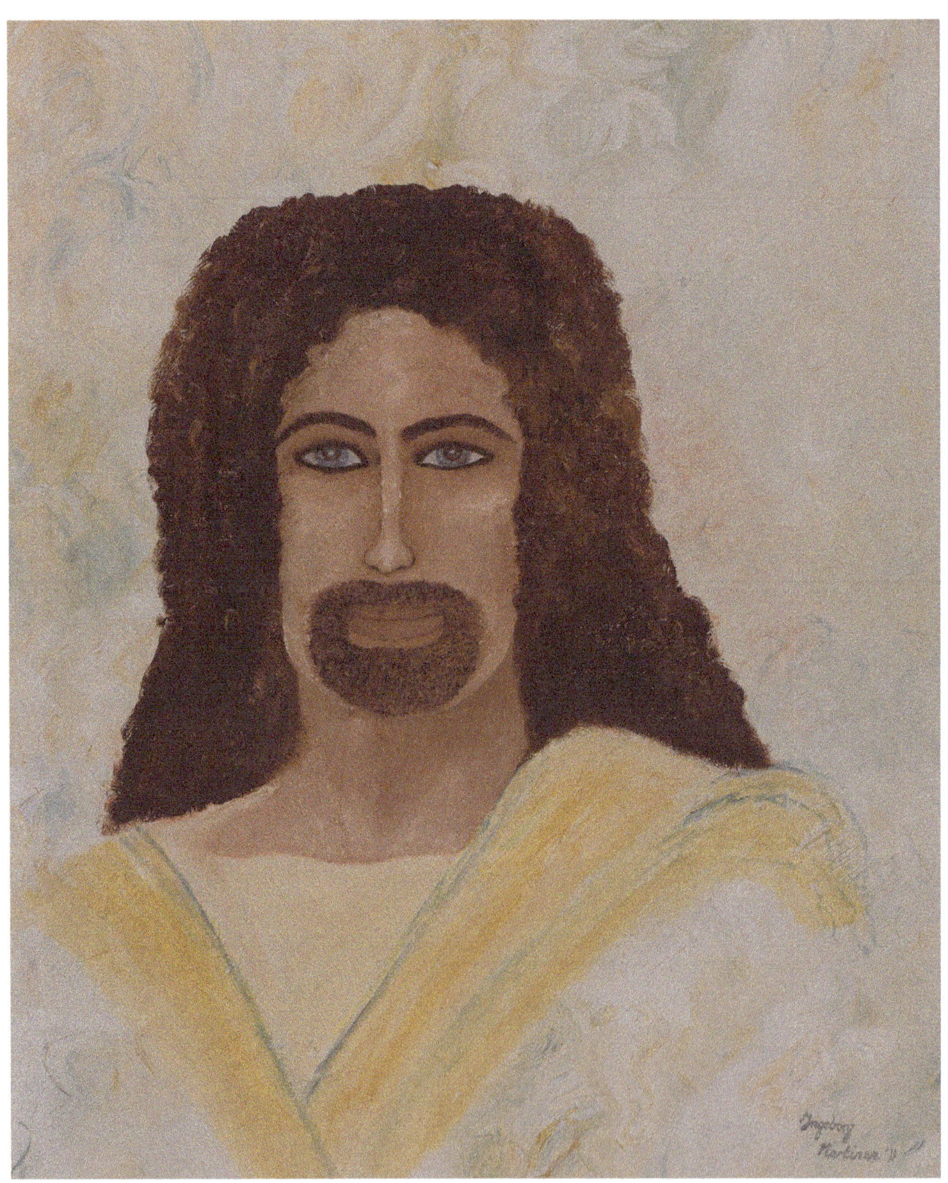

My Presence

Whenever you feel, truly feel My presence,
a deep restful peace showers your soul.
Suddenly there is real joy in your heart.

All the worries of the world are washed away and
for a moment, you are your *Divine Self*.

Seek Me as often as possible;
Increase this *Divine Being* of yours.

See your days in this golden light of divinity and
your daily concerns are dealt with easily.

Ingeborg Martinez

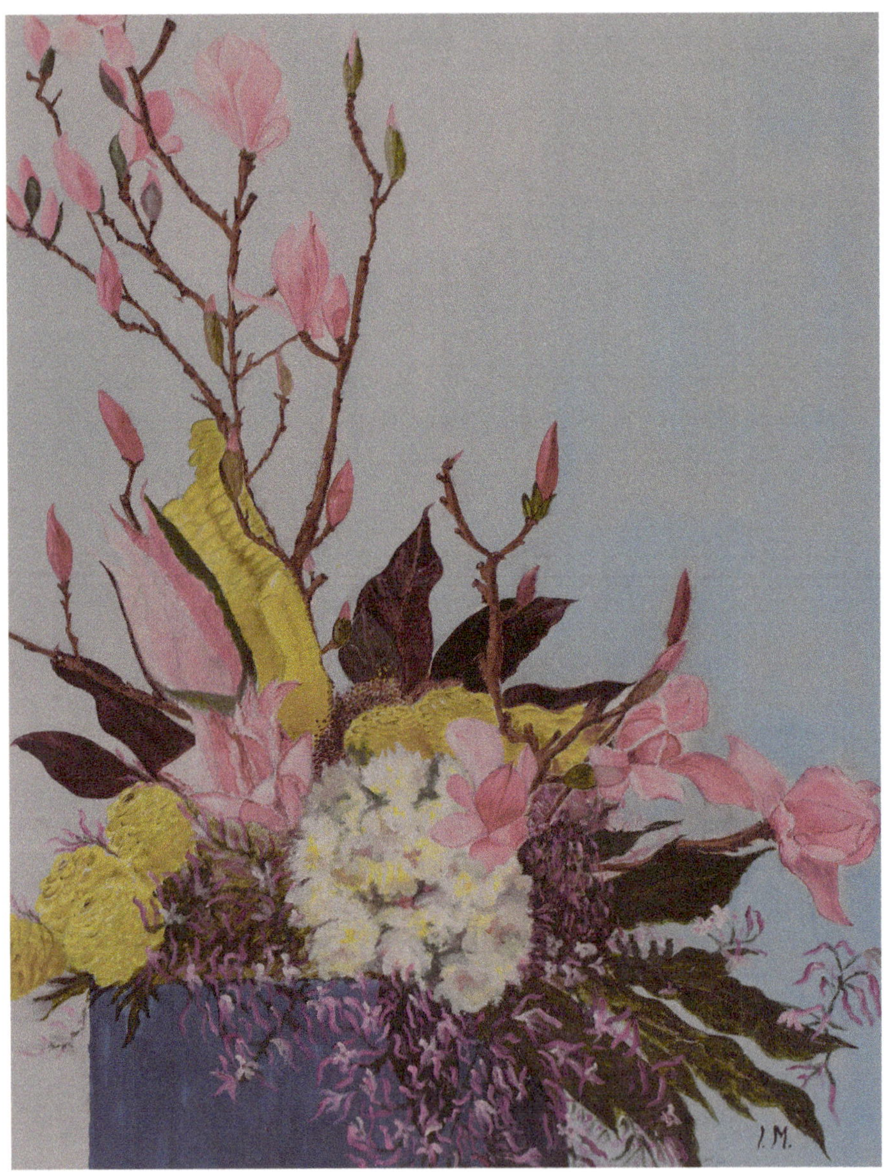

I Am

Nobody can be so close to you as I am!
I am in you, around you and everywhere.

If you hear a song that lifts your heart,
it is ME singing it to you.

If you see a smile that lightens your mood,
it is ME smiling at you.

If you feel love spreading through your whole being,
it is ME, being ONE with you.

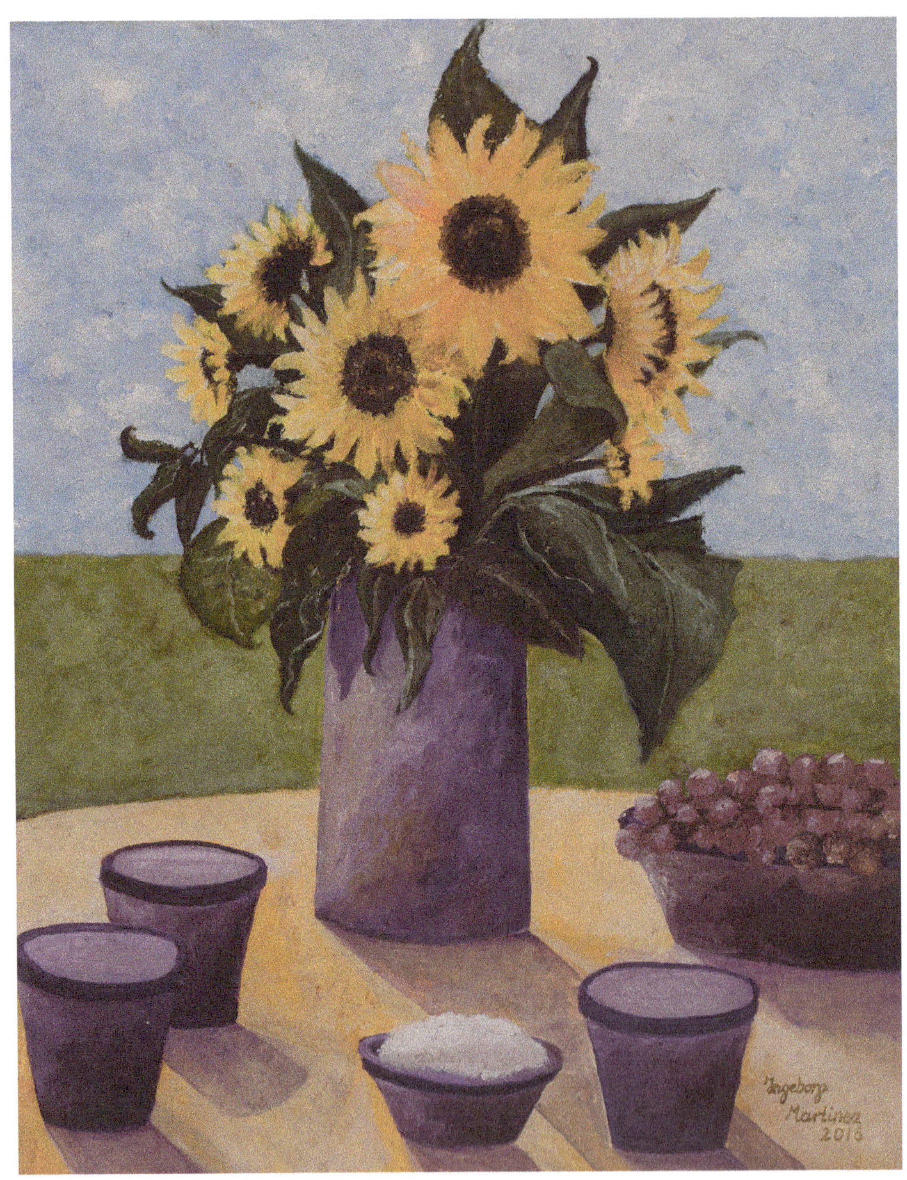

Your True Source

NOW you are truly with ME,
your true source of joy, love and peace.

Nothing in your world is truly lost
but changed into new form.
The level of vibration is what makes
you able to see it with your eyes or
experience it with your other senses.

You are always surrounded by ME
because I am everything:
Every Thing!

That's why to love everything means to love ME.
Your feelings are your guidance.

Negative feelings are needed
to discern the positive.

Bless both and your life will be so much easier!

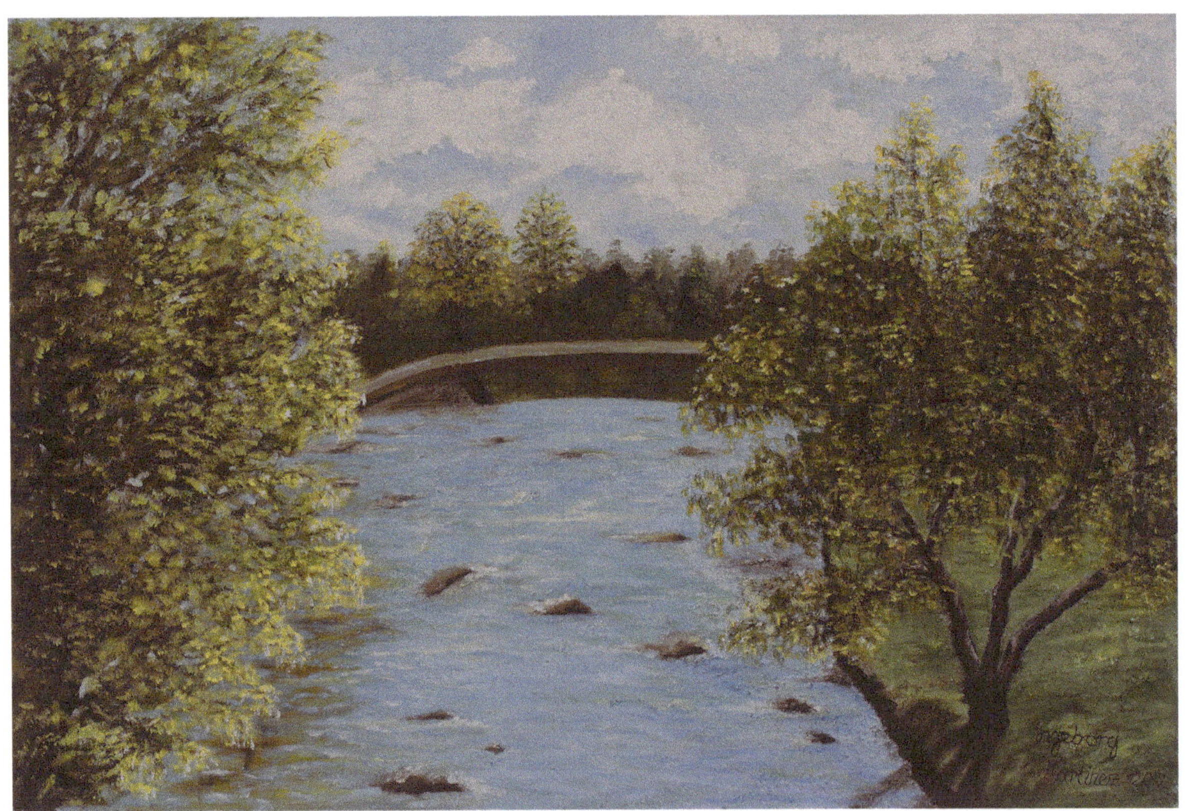

GOD AND FRIEND

GOD Is Your Friend

GOD is the name you use to address ME.
Think of ME as your FRIEND also!

A friend supports, loves and spends time with you.
I do even more:
I spend time with you ALWAYS.
I support you ALWAYS.
I love you ALWAYS.

You think I am only there for you
when you are *godly*.
This is partly true:
I am also there when you are *ungodly*
and love you just the same.

That's what is meant with unconditional love,
support and time.
That is who I AM!

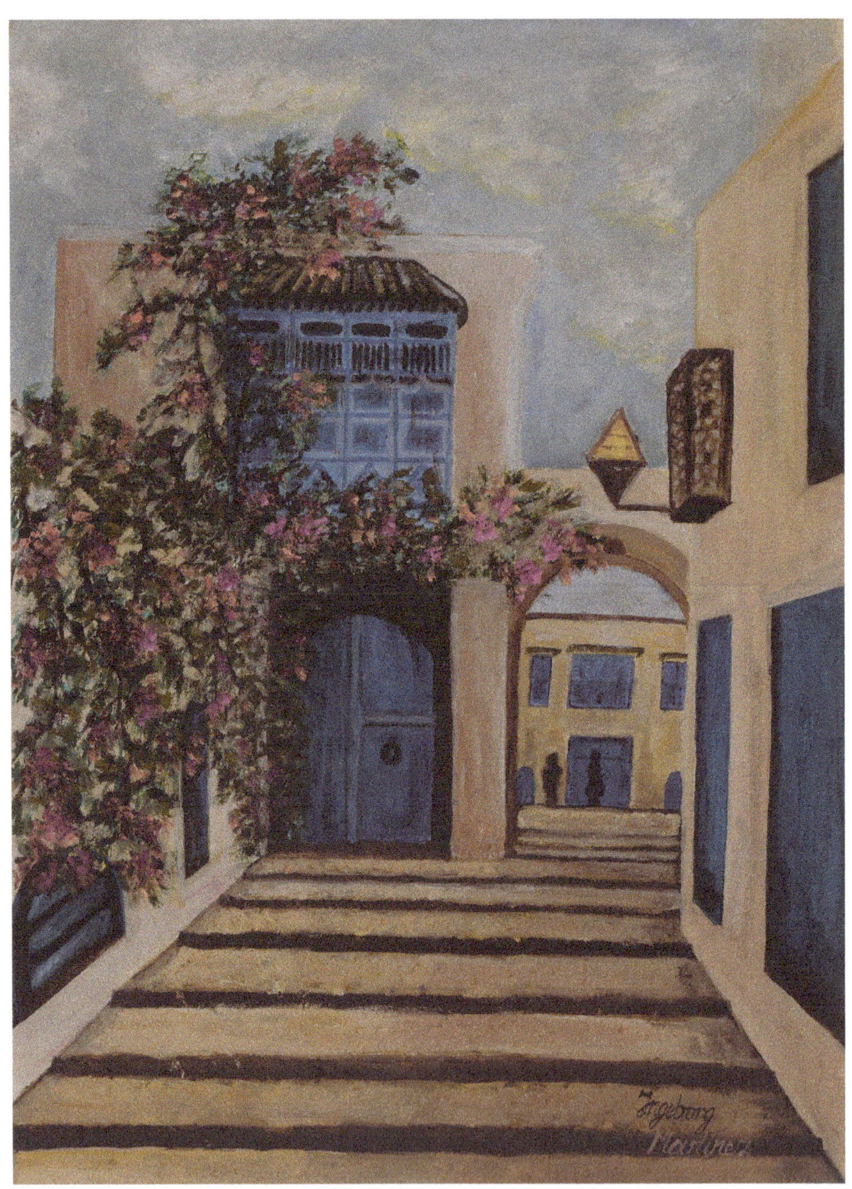

GOD'S MERCY

Mercy

Mercy is a term not completely understood
in the tangles of human relationships.

Nothing is more complicated than
a cluttered and closed mindset.

There is Mercy in each act of Forgiveness
on your part.
This replenishes not only the other's soul
but mostly your own.

Spend your day Forgiving and
granting Mercy and
you have spent it wisely!

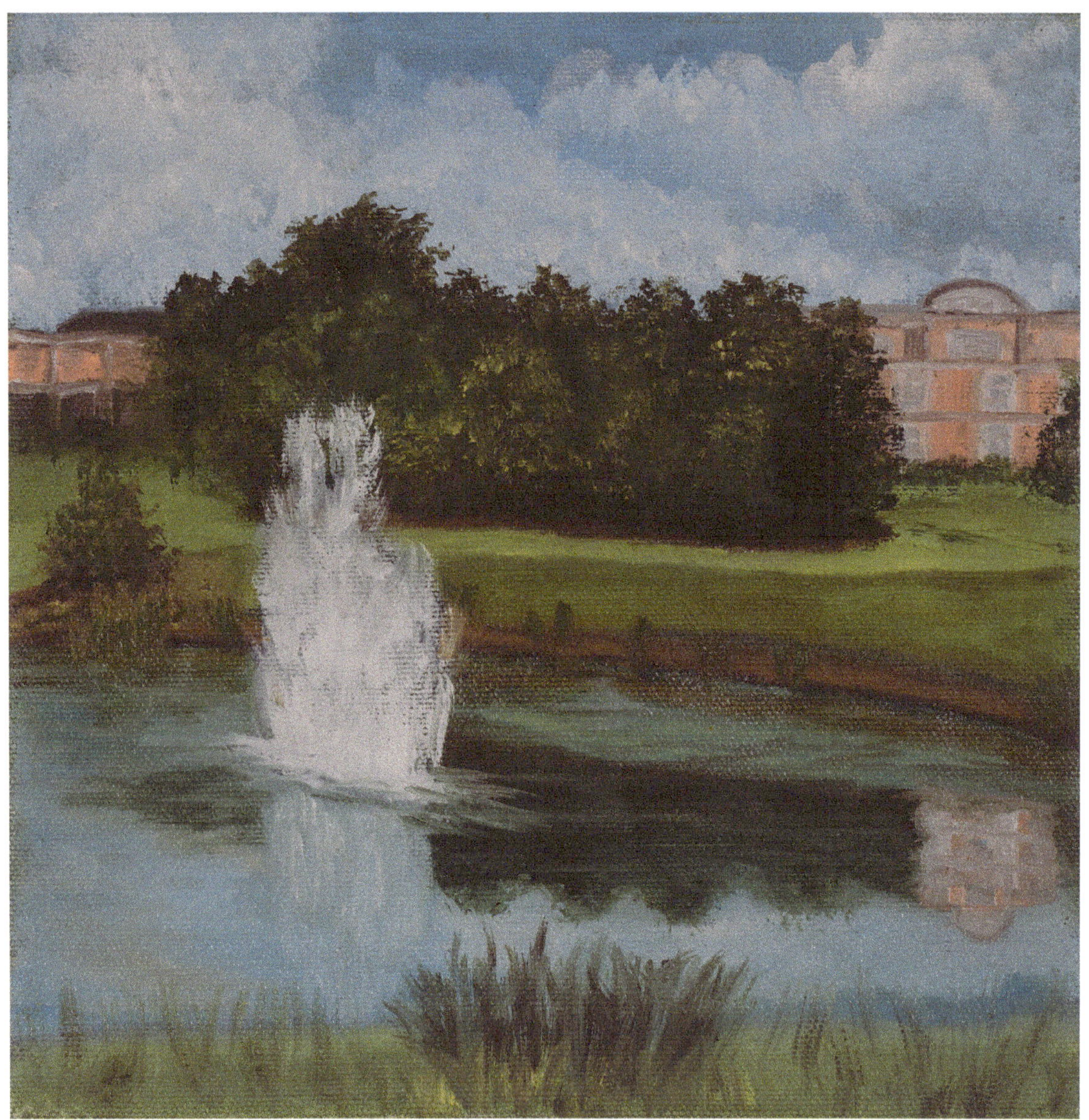

Be Near to ME

Your desire to be near to ME
springs forth from your eternal soul.

You and I are connected forever.
Seemingly being apart in the dimension of time,
making you *think* to have
been torn apart from ME.

You are *never* separated from ME!

Time does not exist.
Eternity does!

You and I are One,
Now and forever!

Notes

Pumpkin Time in Raleigh on page 28
Text: "I Love You Forever"
Oil on canvas, 16" x 20" - 2011
Subject: House entrance in Raleigh, North Carolina
It was the month of October and while walking leisurely through downtown Raleigh, I saw many beautifully decorated houses in fall motifs and colors. Incredibly enchanted, I had to take photos. One special photo was so intriguing that I had to paint the sturdy, red brick entrance surrounded by fall flowers and pumpkins.

Beach Chairs and Sand Pipers on page 30
Text: "A Love Letter from GOD"
Oil on canvas, 20" x 16" – 2004
Subject: Beach scene
Using soft, impressionistic colors, I wanted to create a peaceful scene sitting at the beach.

Mums in a Basket on page 32
Text: "True Love"
Oil on canvas, 16" x 20" – 2012
Subject: Mums
Using vibrant oil colors, I wanted to paint mums as real as possible. Each petal and leaf is painted in detail. I thoroughly enjoyed doing it and admire the finished product.

Heavenly Eyes on page 34
Text: "My Presence"
Oil on canvas, 24" x 20" – 1999
Subject: Jesus
To express my gratitude for the teachings and guidance of our Master "Jesus Christ," I decided to paint his face as I see it: with "Heavenly Eyes."

Beauty in Flowers – I on page 36
Text: "I Am"
Oil on canvas, 22" x 28" – 2002
Subject: Exotic flowers
In the early years of my paintings, I was interested in painting with as much detail as possible, even though the exotic flowers shown in this image are a fantasy seen through my eyes.

Glowing in the Sun on page 38
Text: "Your True Source"
Oil on canvas, 16" x 20" – 2016
Subject: Sunflowers in Vase
Sunflowers make a fabulous subject because they are so vibrant in their yellow/orange expressions. Here I decided to paint them placed in a vase on a table surrounded by fruit and china.

Whispers of Summer on page 40
Text: "God is Your Friend"
Oil on canvas, 36" x 24" – 2012
Subject: Downtown Greenville, South Carolina
Who would have expected to find such a gorgeous view in the middle of a big town? This is what I experienced while attending a three-day bicycle race with my son in Greenville, South Carolina. We had a marvelous time, gorgeous weather, delicious food and after the event I was able to turn a photo into a memorable painting.

Summer in Tunisia on page 42
Text: "Mercy"
Oil on canvas, 12" x 16" – 1996
Subject: Street in the town of Sidi Bou Said, Tunisia
In the year 1996, while on vacation in Tunisia, we booked a day tour with a bus through the country and stopped at the town of Sidi Bou Said. It is located in the north of Tunisia on the top of a steep cliff overlooking the Mediterranean Sea. The town is not only a famous tourist attraction but also an artist community known to have housed famous painters like Paul Klee. The location is absolutely gorgeous. I had an Arabic espresso with pastry on the terrace of one of the coffee shops on the cliff side. The experience was not only breathtakingly beautiful but also delicious.

Meadowmont Fountain on page 44
Text: "Be Near to ME"
Oil on canvas, 8" x 8" – 2015
Subject: Lake at Meadowmont, Chapel Hill, North Carolina
Strolling around in the shopping area of Meadowmont, I turned a corner behind all the buildings and found myself standing amongst lucious greenery and a lake with a beautiful fountain in the middle. What a marvelous, recreational area! I had to take photos and one turned into a small painting.

Chapter 3

Human Emotions

Grief

Grief over Loss

Letting go of the Past

Despair

Do not Despair

Daily Struggles

Despair Not

Anger

Forgiveness

Anger

Fear

Fear of Loss

Pain

Human Pain

Relieve from Pain

Ingeborg Martinez

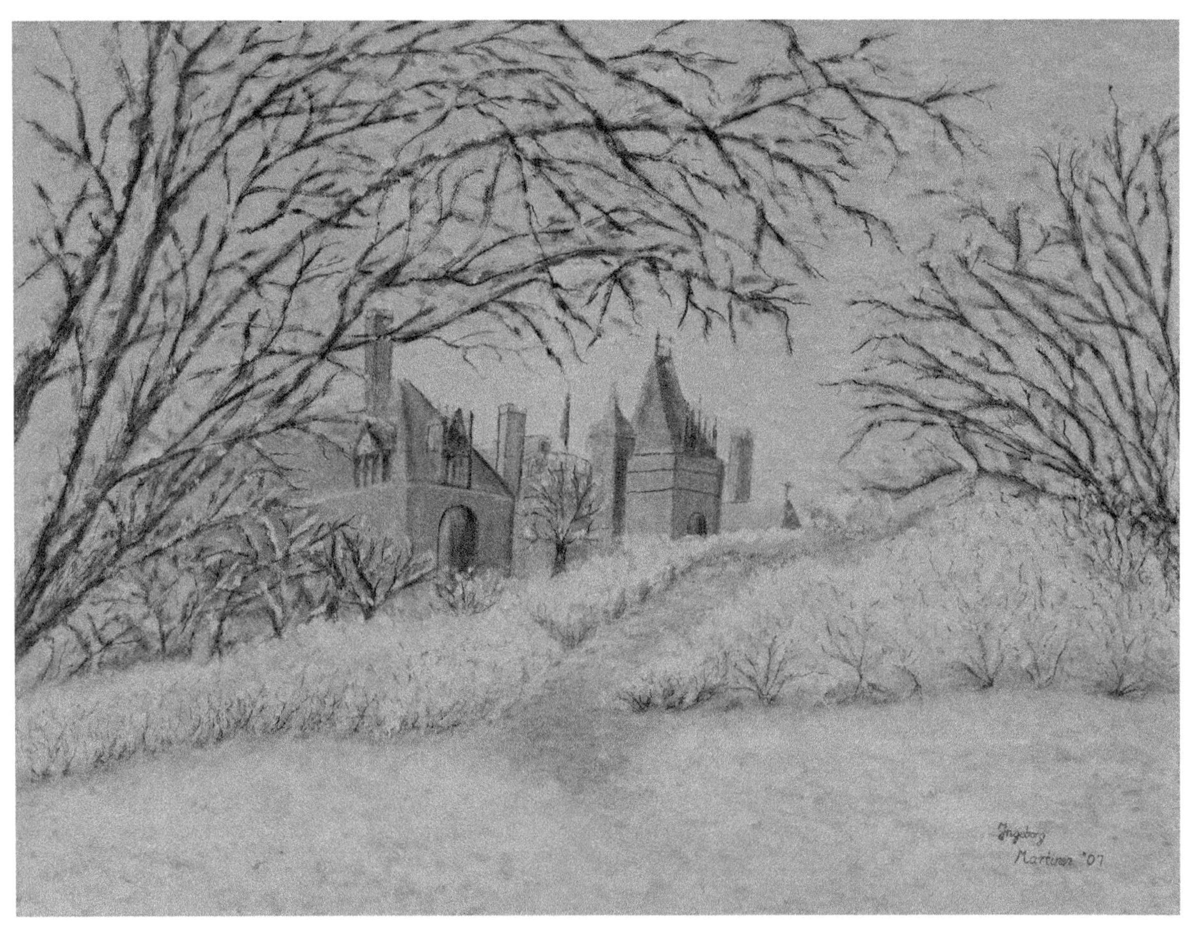

Grief over Loss

Pain, loss, grief.
Grave, darkness, light, understanding, regret.
Blindness, shock, foolishness, tears.

My darling!
Your light blinds my soul.
Your love is balsam.
Your attention is pure sweetness.

How could I have known?
Imprisoned by darkness, surrounded by temptation,
Selfish and ambitious.
I am so, so, so sorry!

I am wishing for you to be carried on
loving hands for the rest of your life.
You are the most glorious butterfly in My garden.
All the sweet words that I never said to you
while alive are now burdening My soul.

I loved you dearly!
But my circumstances were hindering
and I was unconscious.
Please accept my true love for you now!
Of course, I will let you be free.
Though please understand my own foolishness
has hindered the way.

We will see each other again and
by then I am asking for your forgiveness.

Ingeborg Martinez

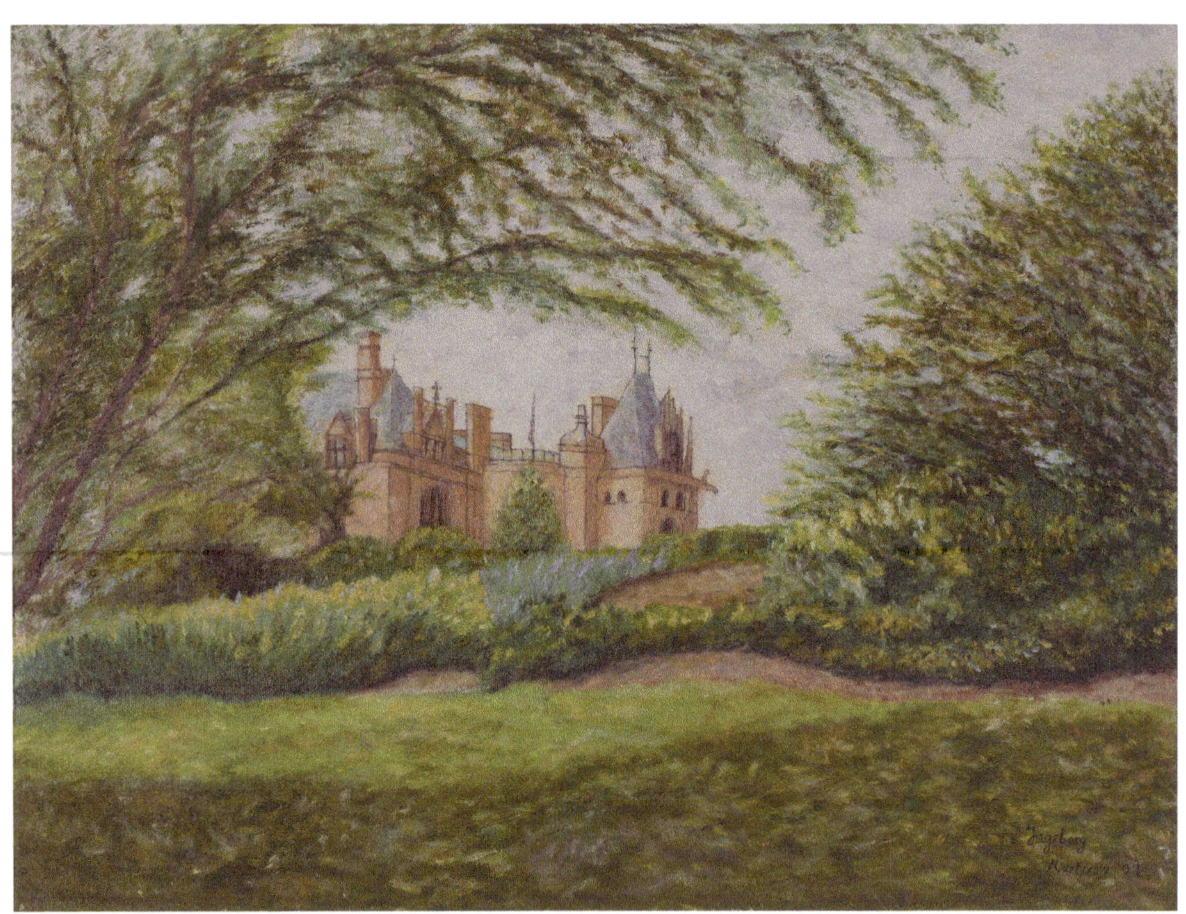

Letting Go of the Past

All your apprehensions are ghosts of the past.
Let them go in peace because they
are completely unfounded.

The guiding posts are erected and all
your wishes will come true.
Now you are able to look forward to
a peaceful and stable life full of love.

All your talents are ready to blossom and
you are highly appreciated and acknowledged.

Let go of the grief over people who
are not able to appreciate you.
This grief is a blockage and hinders your growth.

The answer is *forgiveness*.
Call on your spirit guides and angels for help.
Ask them to keep unkindness away from you.

Ingeborg Martinez

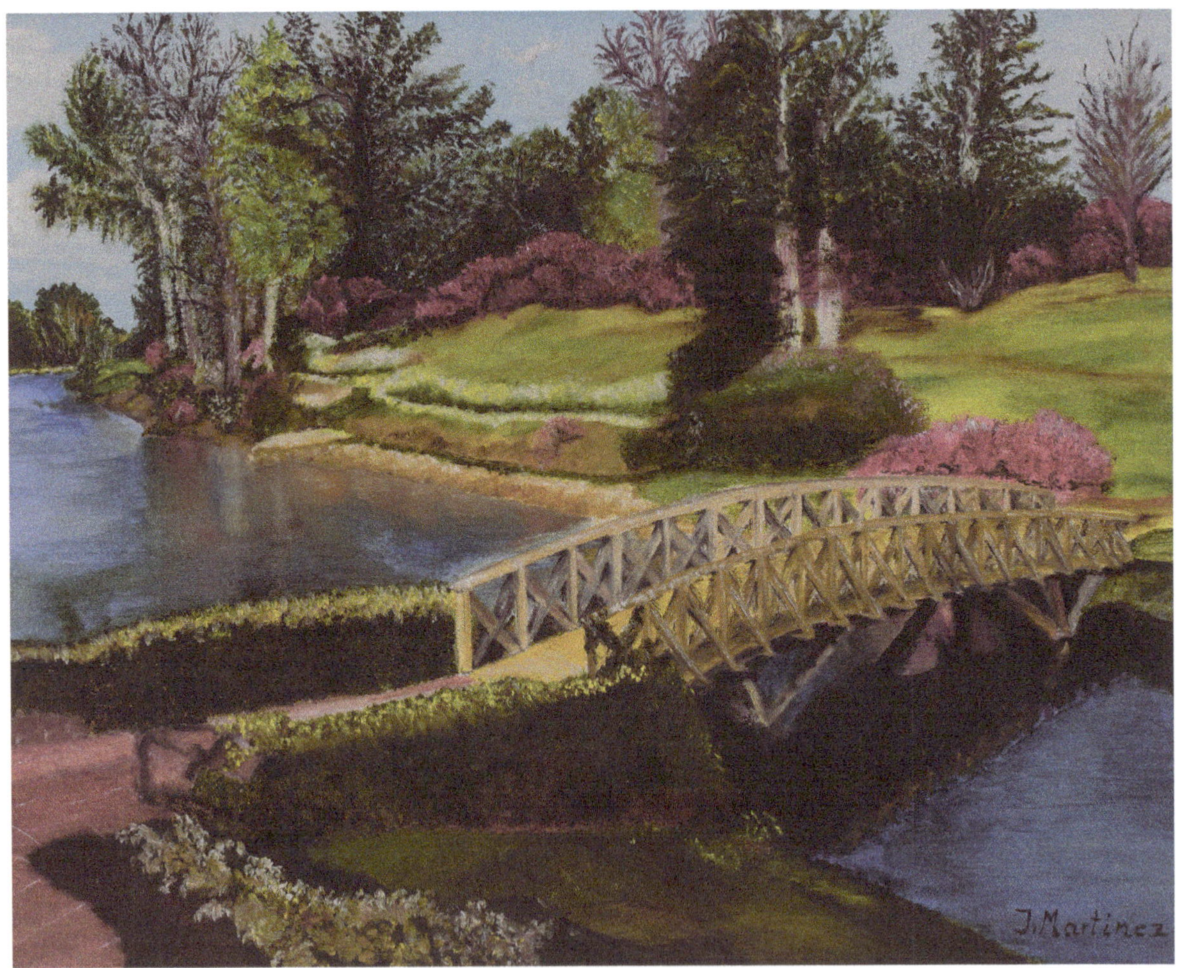

Do Not Despair

Desperation is a downward spiral
for your spirit.
Love is never desperate!
Love is patient and grateful for the NOW.

Be grateful for who you are and
what you have.

You are the rightful king/queen of your
own universe and it sparkles
with love and beauty.

You are the most precious soul,
loved and cherished for eternity.
You are constantly protected and guided.

Do not despair because
everything is as planned.

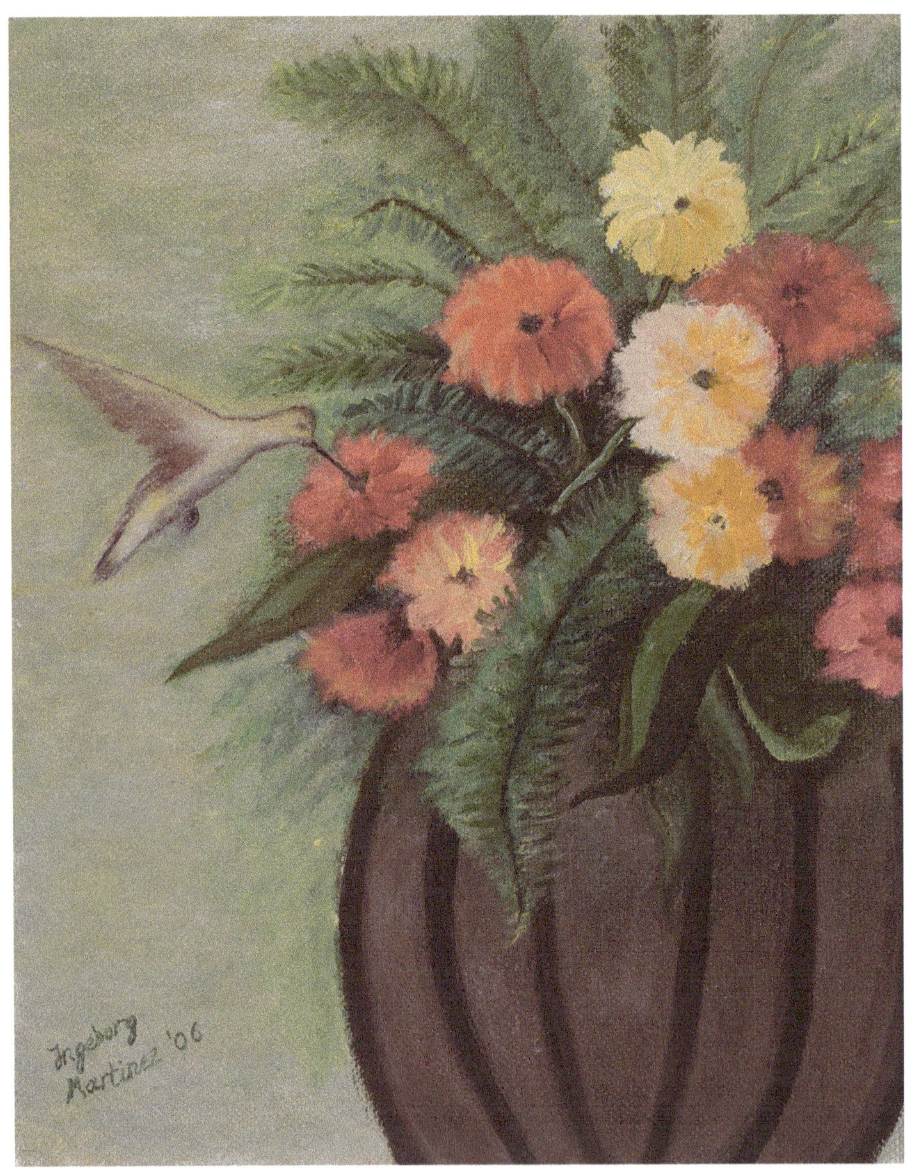

Daily Struggles

Sometimes your will to survive your
daily struggles is contaminated by
negative thinking patterns.

Imagine your life as one filled with joy
no matter what the circumstances are.

Joy and gratefulness fill your soul with
truth and everything that happens
is made *survivable.*

Don't give in to despair and self-pity but
see each encounter as a blessing
brought down from heaven.

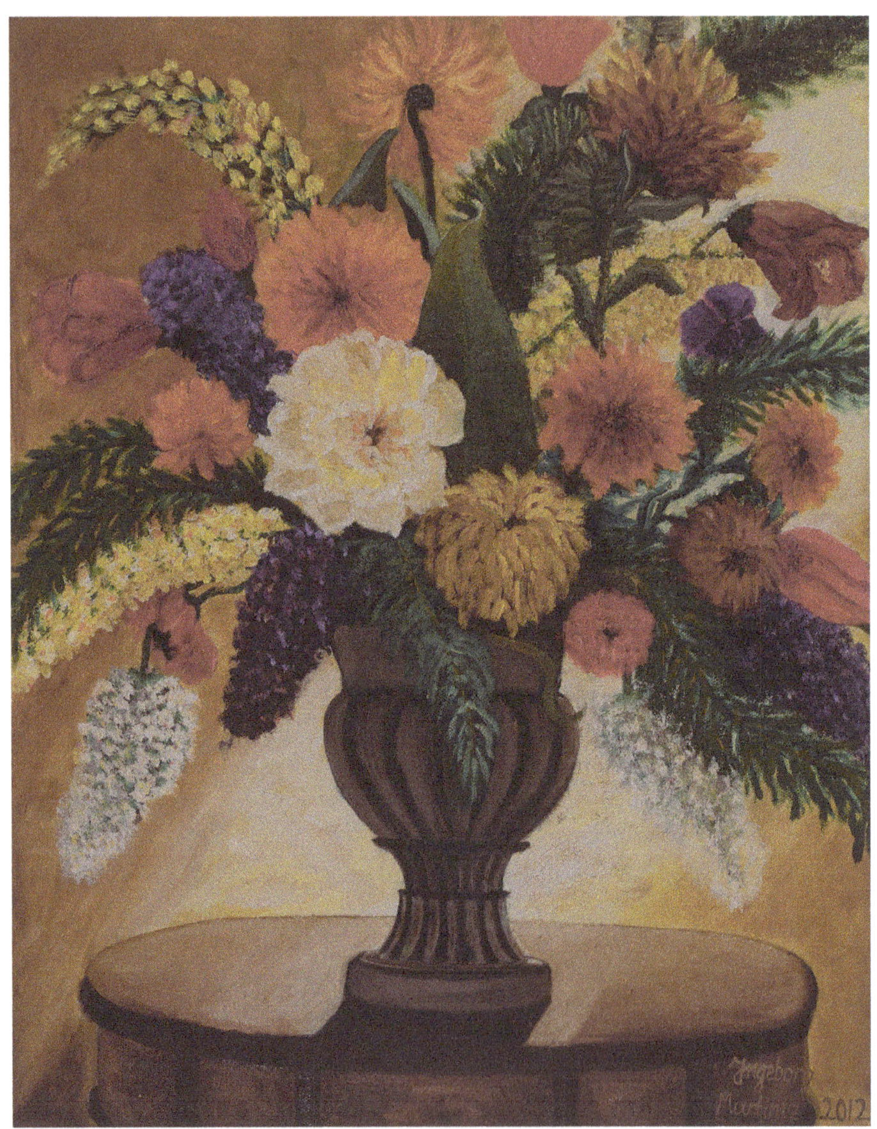

Despair Not

Never give into despair!
It will rob you of all your joy and
leave you empty and dry.

The minute you feel despair coming
your way, immediately call on ME!

Give your feelings into my loving hands.

I will turn them around and soon joy
in your heart will be restored!

Ingeborg Martinez

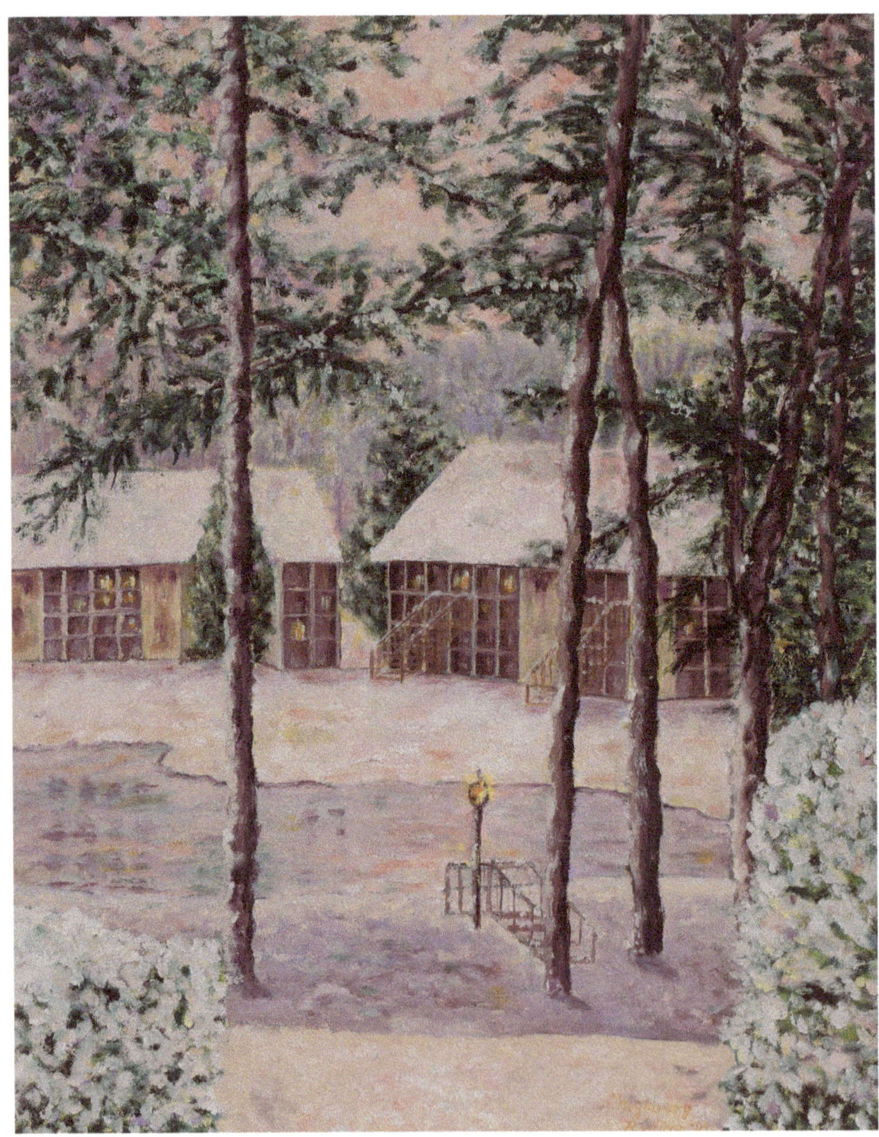

Forgiveness

Anger eats you up inside and out.
You are downtrodden over the unkindness
you have experienced in your life.

Your soul is very strong, but your weakness is
the unkindness you give to your own soul.
Love yourself always including your mistakes.

You are an extremely kind person, but if this
kindness is not returned you react with anger!
You think you are right,
but this is not so!

Unkindness gets stronger with anger.
Your pain increases.
Only forgiveness can deliver you from this pain!

Glued by anger, unkindness stays in
your energy field to make you miserable.

Forgiveness unglues this heavy energy and
sends it out into the universe to
be healed and cleansed.
Your energy field keeps its harmony.
That's why it is so important to release bitterness.

Ingeborg Martinez

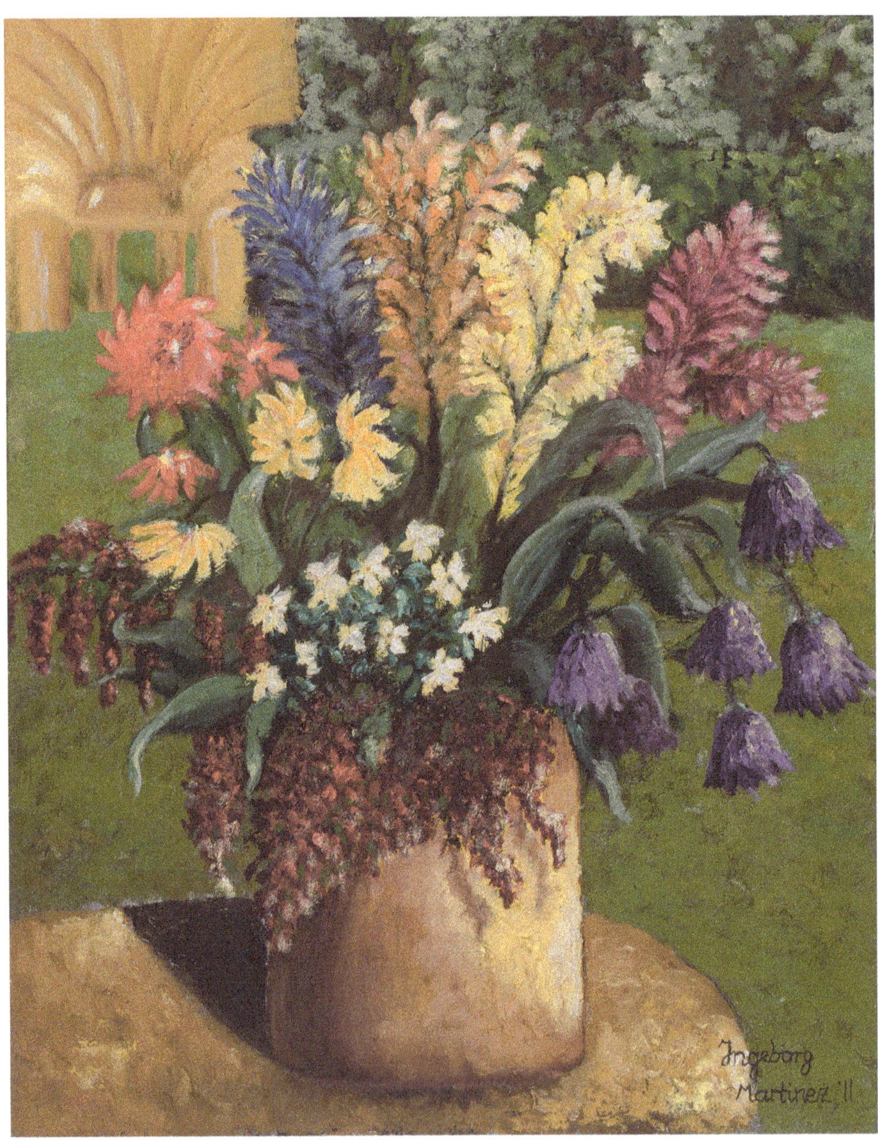

Anger

My beloved child,

You have lessons to learn, therefore you
need the right people around you so that
they can help you to learn them.

Your anger comes from a feeling of
not being loved and appreciated.
Your heart yearns for
acknowledgement and being safe.

You lack trust in ME, your Creator!
You need to learn you are deeply loved
by ME and no outside appearances
can give this to you.

Trusting in ME is a hard lesson to learn and it takes
a lot of bravery to *Let go and let GOD!*
You are on your way to trusting in ME more and more.
The more you trust in ME, the less angry and
dependent on others' approval you will be.

Joy is already replacing all your negative
thoughts and you are becoming calmer.
I love you dearly and I am always,
always with you.

I bless you in abundance and
know your day to be marvelous.

The Divine

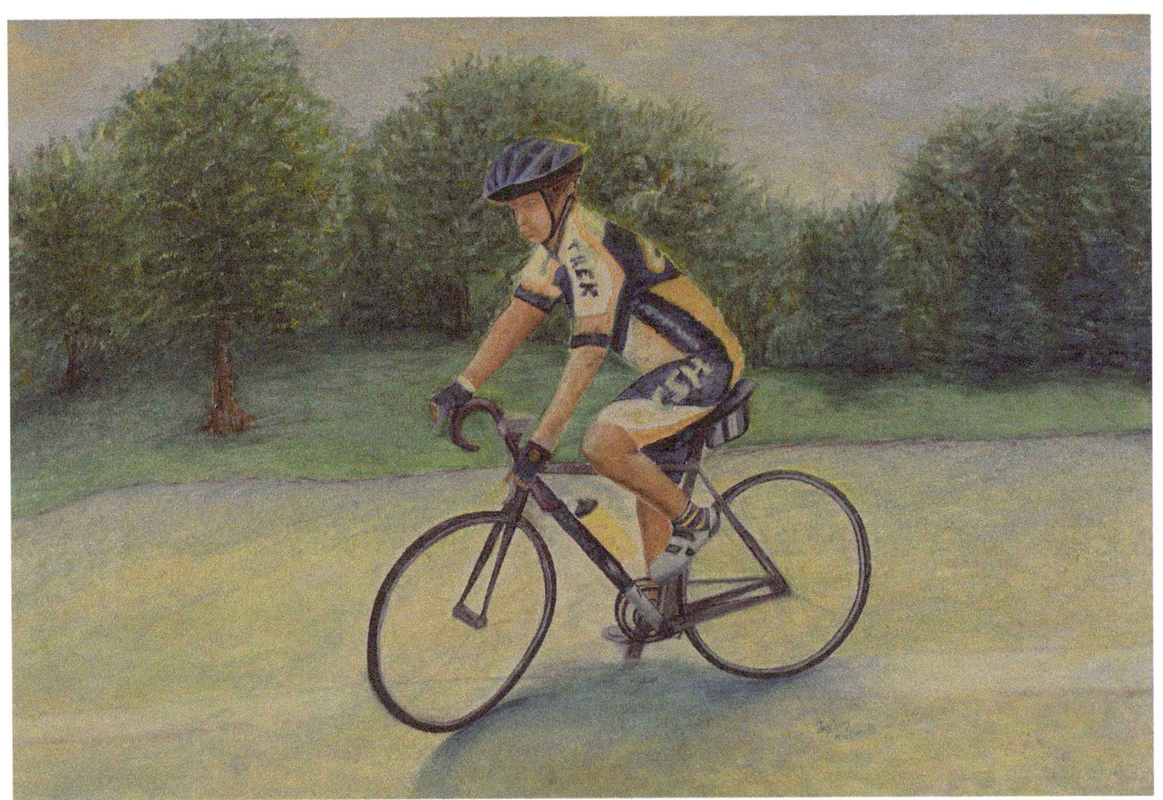

Fear of Loss

Your ego is in overdrive.
It is highly upset because its needs are not met.

Inside yourself is a deep knowing
that you are doing the right thing,
but your ego is scared of losing it all.

Now, to calm your ego, you have to be brave.
You are determined to do the right thing
and this will eventually calm down your ego.

Give it time and you will know this day will end
peacefully and with a sense of accomplishment.

You are a brave soldier and
we are very proud of you!

We guard you constantly and
everything is in order.

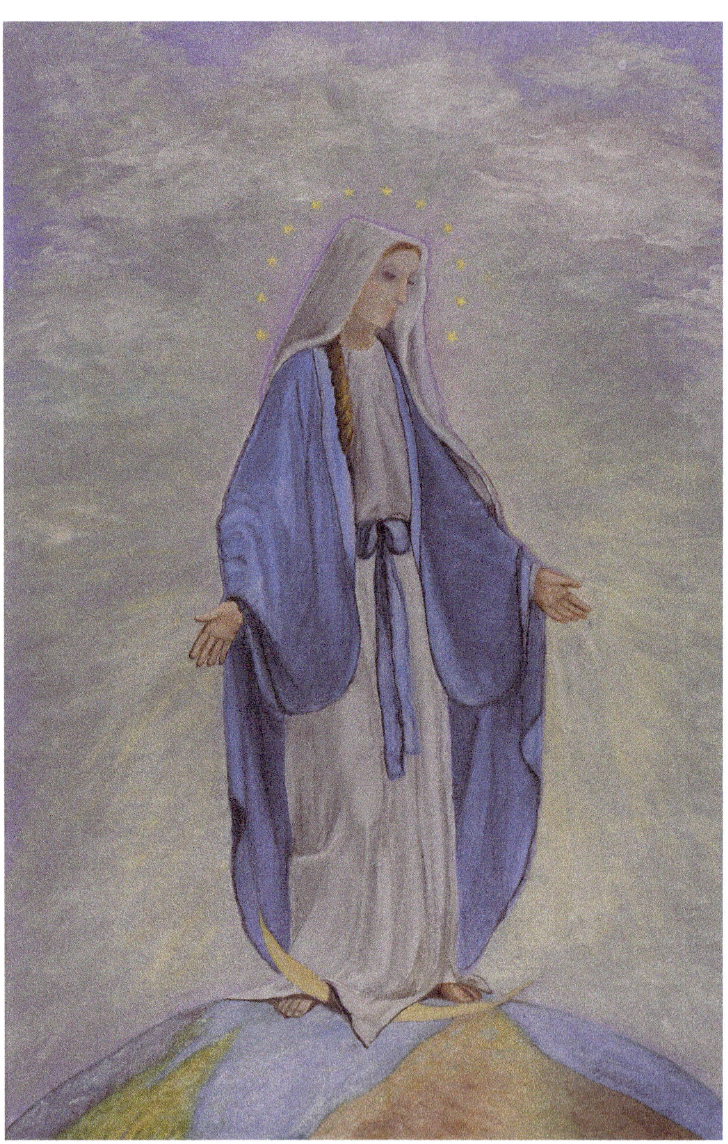

Human Pain

You are vulnerable as a human being and
the hurts inflicted upon you are plenty.

But there is good news found in your ordeal:
I am with you and I am aware of your pain.

If you open your heart and let me in,
I will ease this burden.

Trust in ME, your real friend,
and your sorrows will fade away.

Ingeborg Martinez

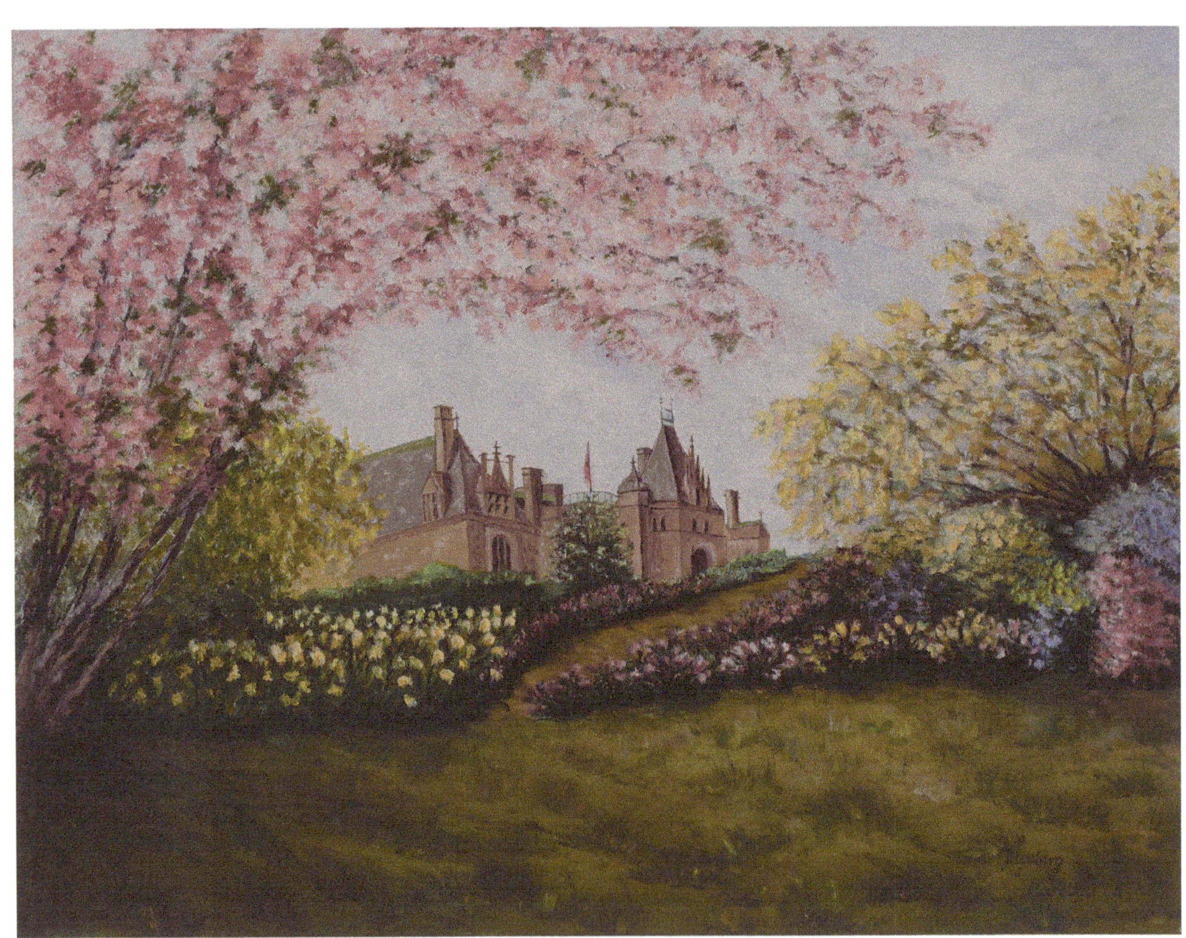

Relief from Pain

Under the influence of us, your guides,
you move straightforward on your path.

As you look on your life now,
there is only contentment.

We are extremely proud of you!

Your intuition is getting stronger and stronger,
although we are sorry for your pain.

We will help you to get relief from this pain
in a professional and healthy way.

We promise you will be able to move around
and enjoy your life even more.

Notes

Biltmore Estate in Winter on page 50
Text: "Grief over Loss"
Oil on canvas, 24" x 18" – 2008
Subject: Biltmore Estate, Asheville, North Carolina
This motif is the subject for four identical paintings, each set in the four seasons. Travels for bicycle races brought us close to Asheville, North Carolina several times. Visiting Biltmore Estate a couple of times resulted in many beautiful photos. This particular perspective of the estate was captured out of the adjacent gardens.

Biltmore Estate in Summer on page 52
Text: "Letting Go of the Past"
Oil on canvas, 24" x 18" – 2008
Subject: Biltmore Estate, Asheville, North Carolina
See description for previous painting
Same perspective set in summer colors.

The Foot Bridge on page 54
Text: "Do Not Despair"
Oil on canvas, 20" x 16" – 2005
Subject: Landscape with bridge
With this motif I challenged myself to discover dimensions, light, shade, structure, etc. in painting a wooden foot bridge.

On Light Wings on page 56
Text: "Daily Struggles"
Oil on canvas, 8" x 10" - 2005
Subject: Hummingbird and flowers
This scene is created purely from my imagination as I see a hummingbird feeding off a flower.

Fantasy in Flowers on page 58
Text: "Despair Not"
Oil on canvas, 16" x 20" - 2012
Subject: Flowers on table
A bouquet of flowers evoked a fantasy from my imagination. The light pours from behind illuminating flowers and table.

Winter Light on page 60
Text: "Forgiveness"
Oil on canvas, 16" x 20" - 2009
Subject: Huntington Apartments, Morrisville, North Carolina
Winter Light is one of five paintings with winter motifs. One day, we had a blizzard running through pouring several inches of snow on the ground. Everything was closed and I had the time to walk around the pond in the middle of the complex and take many fabulous photos. Those photos turned into marvelous winter scenes.

Ingeborg Martinez

Splash of Color on page 62
Text: "Anger"
Oil on canvas, 16" x 20" – 2011
Subject: Fantasy Flowers
The flowers are created purely from my imagination. With this painting, I just wanted to bring bright colors onto the canvas without worrying too much about perspective and shade.

Silent Ride on page 64
Text: "Fear of Loss"
Oil on canvas, 36" x 24" – 2006
Subject: My son, Dominic, on his bicycle
To honor bicycle riders who have been victims of an accident with a car and passed away, a special group of bicycle riders hold an annual "Silent Ride." This one was located in Durham, North Carolina, and my son, Dominic, wanted to be part of it to honor the victims.
I took several photos, and as a memory chose this motif to paint him.

Madonna on page 66
Text: "Human Pain"
Oil on canvas, 24" x 36" – 2006
Subject: Mother Mary
To honor our heavenly Mother, I wanted to paint her as she is protecting and watching over all her children on earth.

Biltmore Estate Spring on page 68
Text: "Relief from Pain"
Oil on canvas, 24" x 18" – 2008
Subject: Biltmore Estate, Asheville, North Carolina
One of four paintings set in the four seasons.
See explanation on page 70.

Chapter 4

Healing, Harmony and Balance

Harmony and Balance
> Inner Balance
>
> Healing the Soul
>
> The Bright Star
>
> Divine Self

The Mind
> Calmness of the Mind
>
> The Power of Your Thoughts
>
> Mind – A Powerful Tool
>
> Yesterday

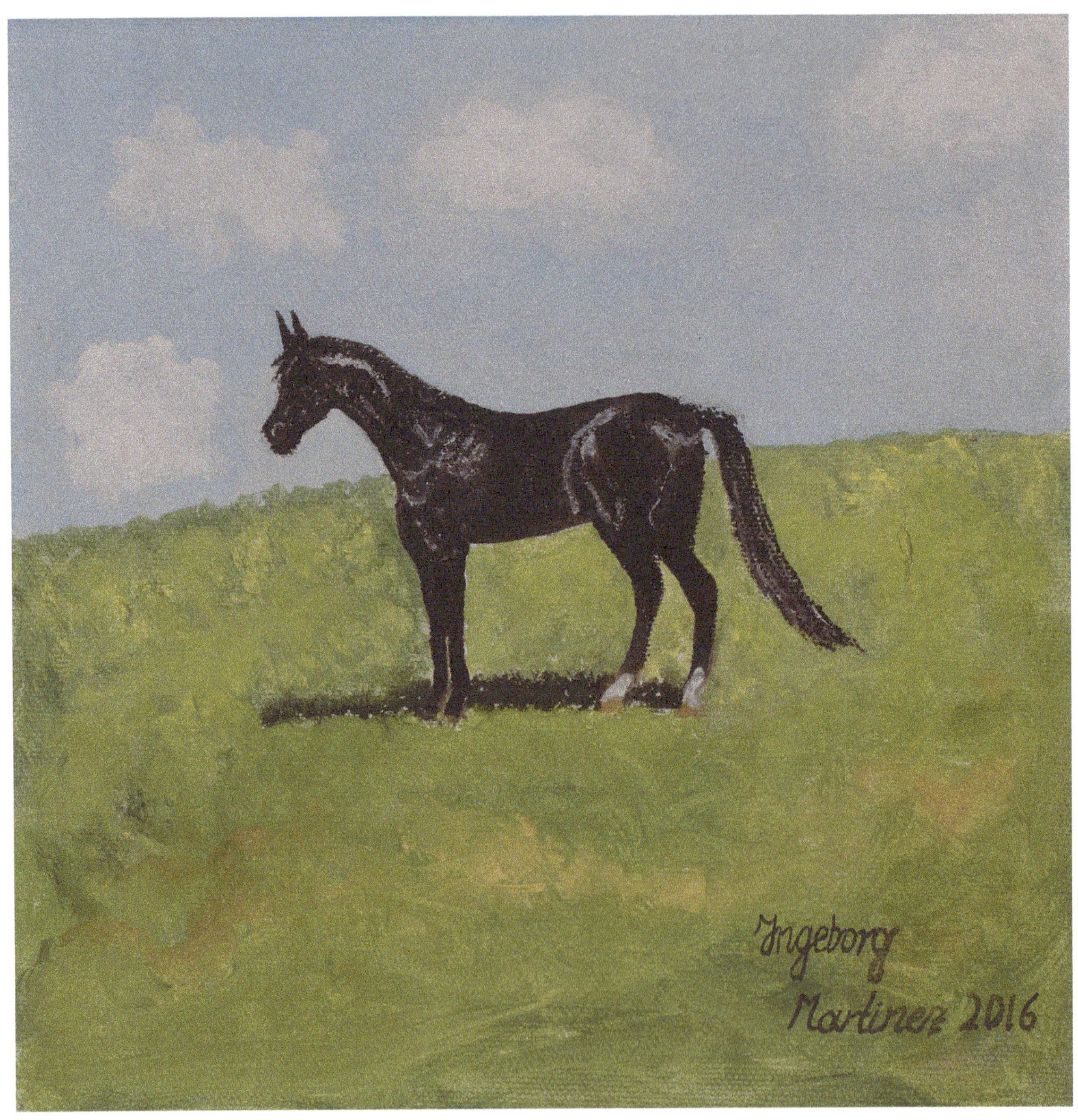

Inner Balance

Nothing is more important than
to keep your inner harmony and balance.

Let My light shine in you and through you.

The warmth of My Light will keep you
loving to yourself and to others.

The smile in your being
illuminates the world around you,
bathing it in My everlasting love and light.

Ingeborg Martinez

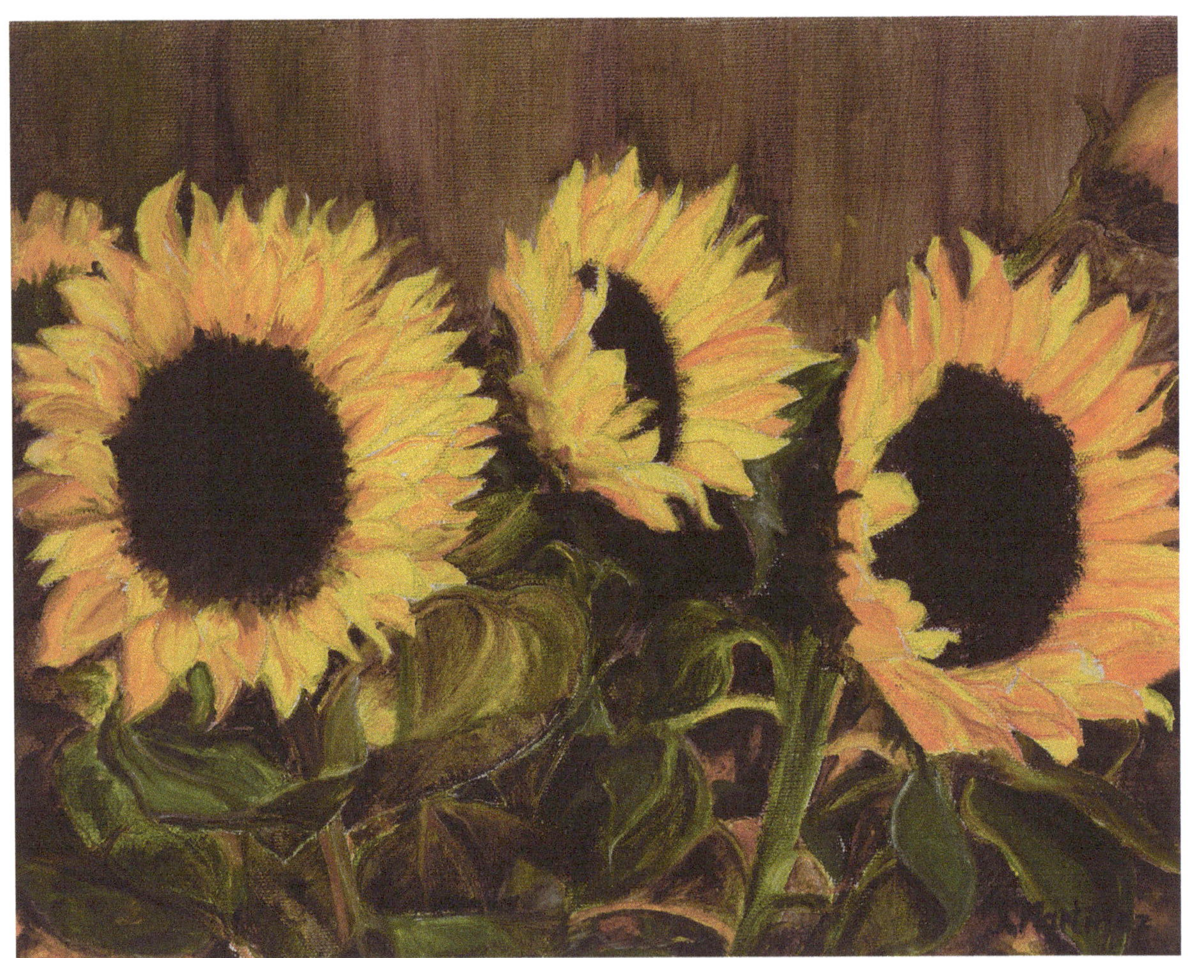

Healing the Soul

To heal means to bring parts back
into your consciousness that are
momentarily hidden in the dark.

Those are things, feelings, persons,
situations and circumstances that
you are afraid of.

Fear is not real, only love is!

As you allow the truth to shine into the parts
that you are afraid of,
fear and untruth disappear and
you heal from the fragmentation.

Healing is water for your soul.
Everything starts to flow freely and
your whole being starts to expand.

Ingeborg Martinez

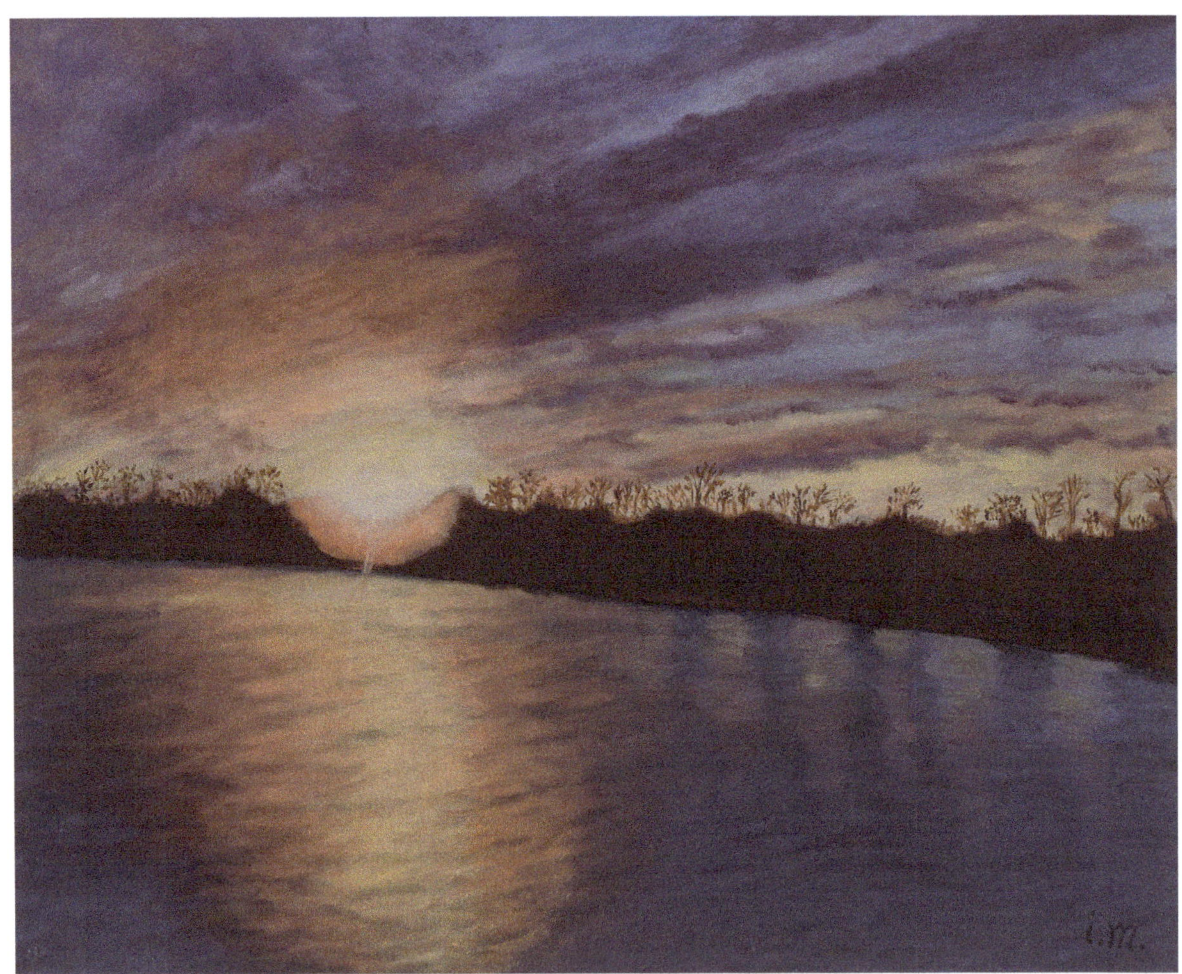

The Bright Star

Over the moon there is a bright star;
Behind the fear is bright light.

You are in a state of healing.
Everything is in order but your mind
is upset and confused.

This is absolutely *Okay*.
Healing is digging into the chaos to release it.

Never think of yourself as minor
or unimportant.

You are a *Bright Star*!
Let yourself shine,
today and every day!

Ingeborg Martinez

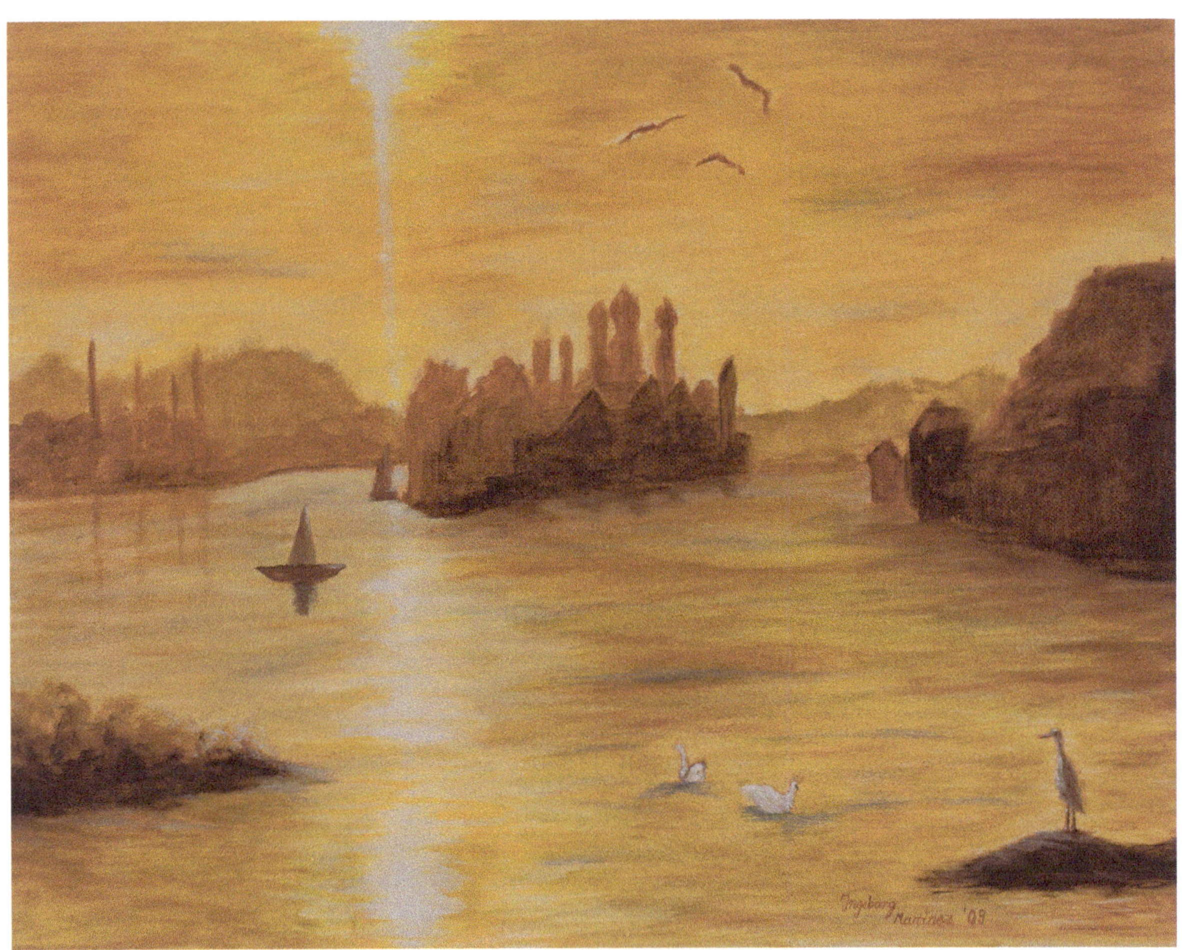

Divine Self

Don't worry about if everything is in perfect order.
Yes, sometimes there seems to be chaos,
but it is only as you see it.

Actually, everything is in perfect order!
Divinely created and guided.

You, yourself are divine perfection,
created in my image.

Your eyes are clouded with illusions,
but mine can see clearly.

I see you in all your splendor,
your true divine self:

Forever shining,
forever bright,
forever loved.

Ingeborg Martinez

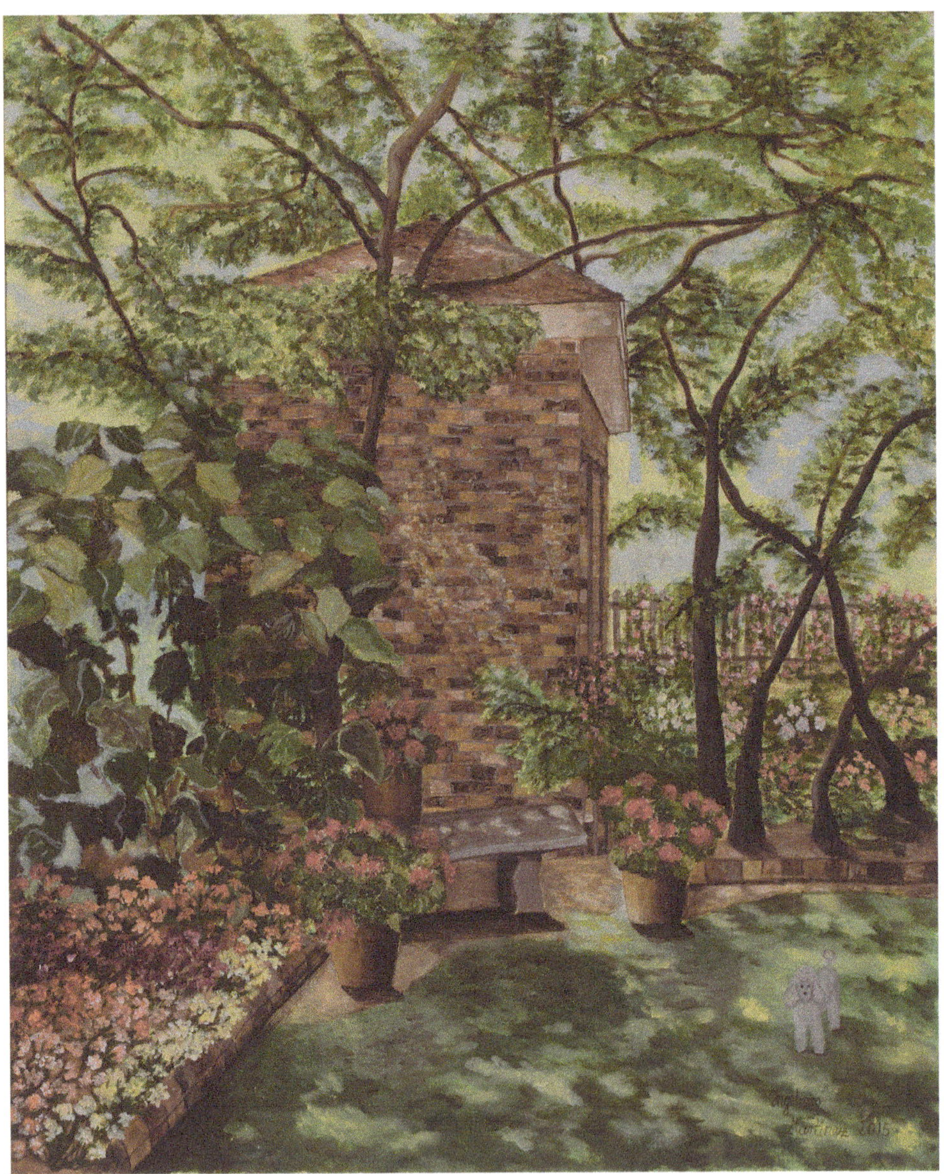

THE MIND

Calmness of the Mind

Calmness of the mind brings
calmness to the whole being.
Where to find this tranquility
but in ME, your Father.

Everything you say and do comes
first out of your mind.
Connect with ME constantly,
especially in times of trouble!

I am your comforter.
I am your peace.
I am your joy.
I am your strength.

I am.
I am.
I am.
And so are You!

Ingeborg Martinez

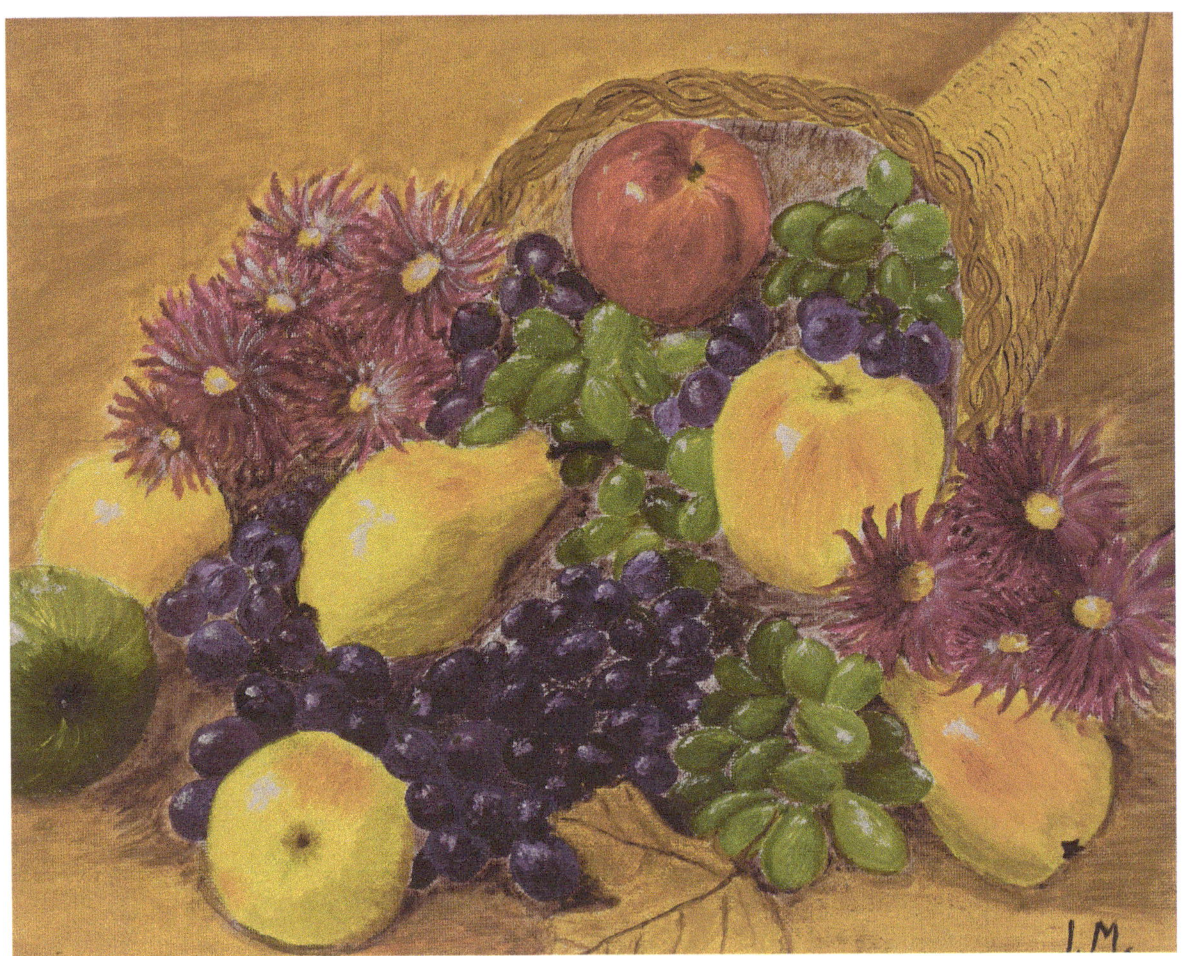

The Power of Your Thoughts

Never underestimate the power
of your own thoughts.

You are what you think.
How you think is how you speak and then act.
Thoughts of inferiority produce a little mind,
keeping yourself trapped in your smaller self.

Change your thoughts and
you will change your life!
Imagine yourself healthy, vibrant and full of life.

Gratefulness, inner joy and love
produce a peaceful life in harmony
with yourself and everything around you.

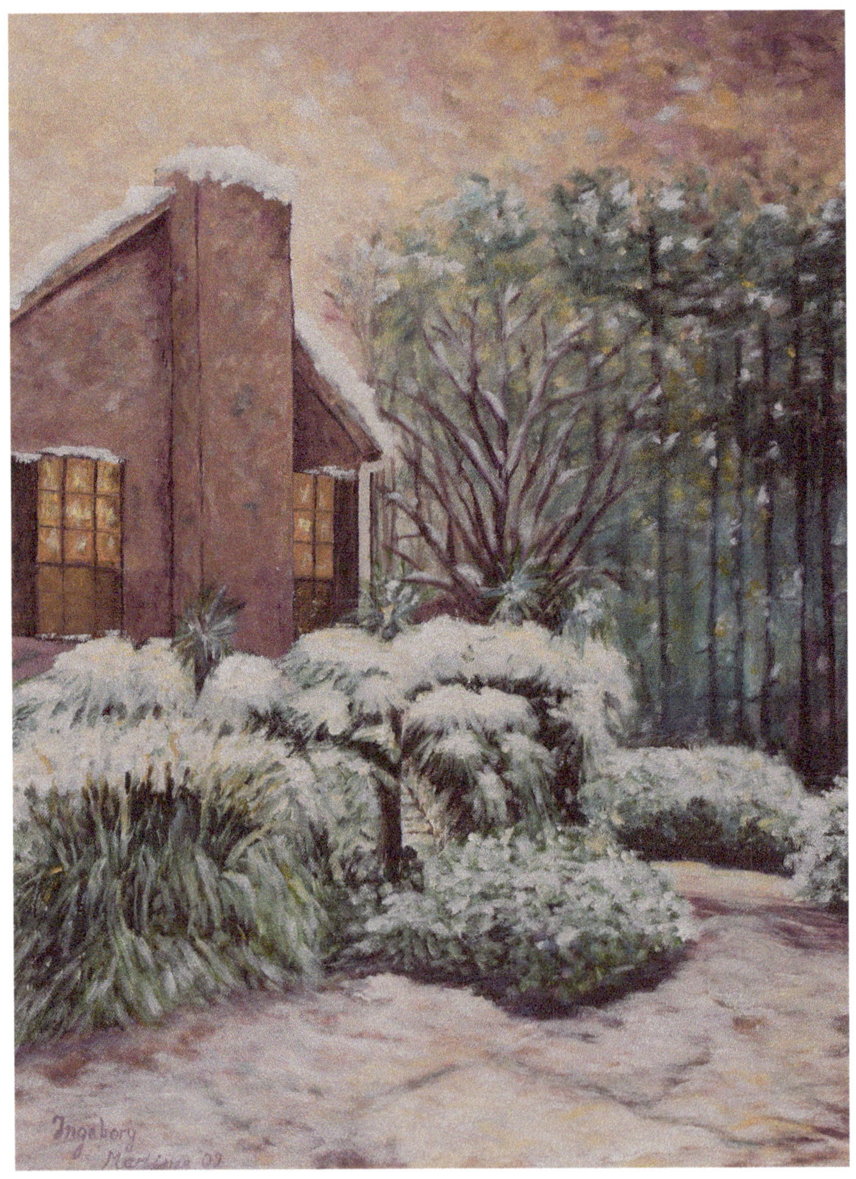

Mind – A Powerful Tool

Your mind is a powerful tool;
Use it wisely!

If your thoughts are directed in a
healthy direction you will create health.

Your intuition is a useful guidance system.
If you have unsettling feelings about anything,
listen to them; they are mostly right.

To make decisions, small or large,
listen first to this Inner Voice.

Peace, love and joy means: Go ahead!

Fear, inner struggle and apprehension means:
Stop and wait!

Ingeborg Martinez

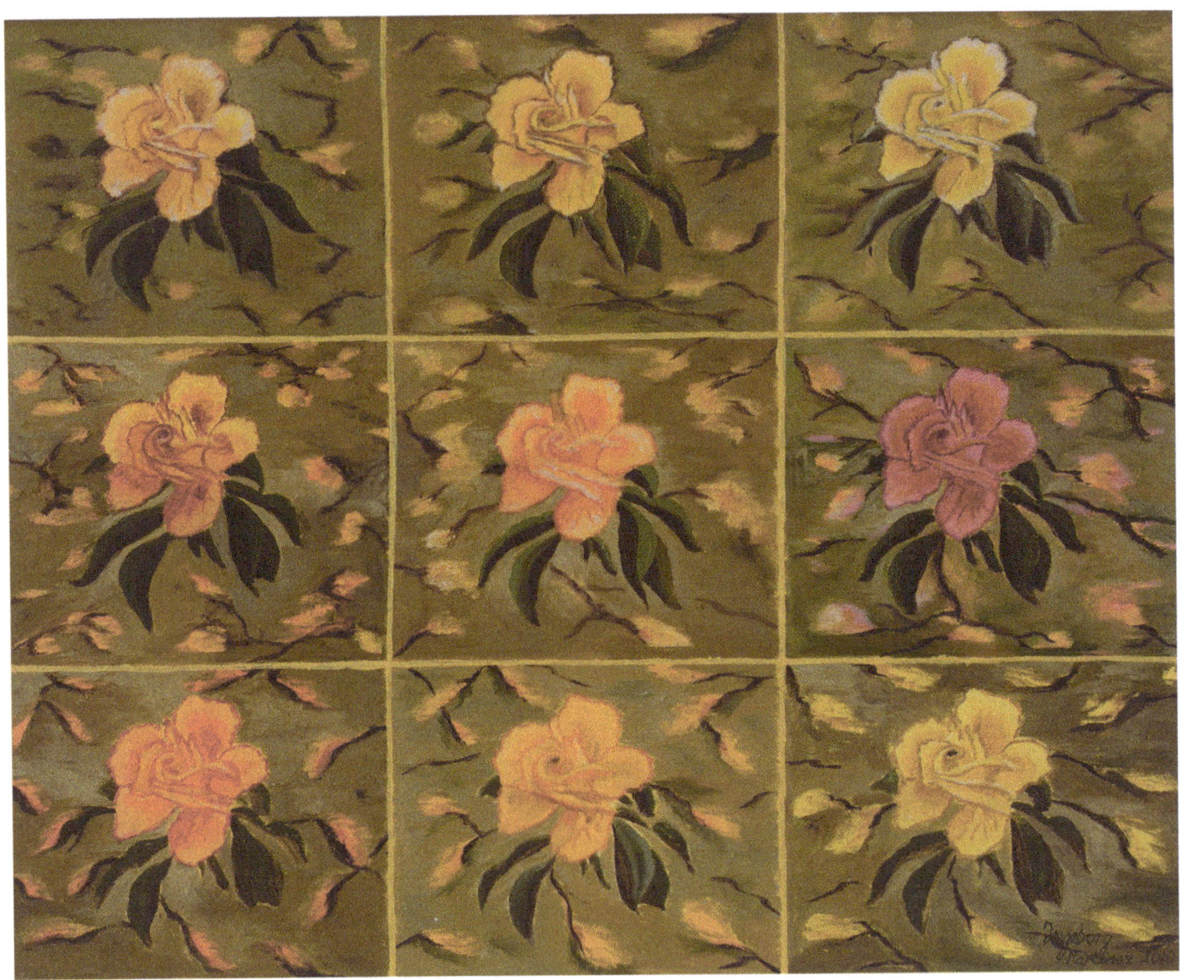

Yesterday

Yesterday was NOT in your mind
after waking up.
You totally forgot everything.

Your body, though, still remembers
the abuse you have been given.

Let it rest!
Let it heal!
Give it grace!

I am with you, always!

Notes

Black Beauty on page 74
Text: "Inner Balance"
Oil on canvas, 8" x 8" – 2016
Subject: A horse
Quickly, I wanted to paint a horse. This is the result: a black horse standing peacefully and content in the meadow.

Shining in the Sun on page 76
Text: "Healing the Soul"
Oil on canvas, 20" x 16" – 2005
Subject: Sunflowers
This is a study of light and shade using sunflowers.

Glowing Sundown on page 78
Text: "The Bright Star"
Oil on canvas, 16" x 20" – 2014
Subject: Cape Fear, Wilmington, North Carolina
Celebrating our 25th wedding anniversary, we strolled along the board-walk in Wilmington, North Carolina in the evening. The colors of the sunset were breathtaking and I took some photos. This painting was done in memory of that special day.

The Golden Beam on page 80
Text: "Divine Self"
Oil on canvas, 14" x 18" – 2009
Subject: Passau, Germany
Passau is a German city in Bavaria and located close to the Austrian border. It is famous for the three rivers that come together at the town: The Danube, Inn and Ilz. My painting shows the confluence of the three rivers. I created this piece from a photo taken during my honeymoon in 1979 riding a sightseeing tour boat in the evening.

Poplar Kitchen on page 82
Text: "Calmness of the Mind"
Oil on canvas, 20" x 24" – 2015
While being on vacation in Wilmington, North Carolina, we went to visit Poplar Grove, a former sweet potato and peanut plantation. In 1980, Poplar Grove Plantation was turned into a museum.
Next to the main building stands a small brick house, which turned out to be the former kitchen. What a beautiful sight it was during the summer time. Seeing one of the several photos taken at the visit, I decided to paint this especially charming brick house surrounded by trees, plants and flowers.

Cornucopia on page 84
Text: "The Power of Your Thoughts"
Oil on canvas, 14" x 11" – 2001
Subject: Fruits and flowers
Who doesn't like to see a cornucopia, representing rich harvest, well-being and wealth? As this is one of our favorite subjects, I too had to joyfully express it on canvas.

Winter at Home on page 86
Text: "Mind – A Powerful Tool
Oil on canvas, 18" x 24" – 2009
Subject: Huntington Apartments, Morrisville, North Carolina
This is another of several winter paintings. Explanation can be found on page 71.

Ingeborg Martinez

Slow Down and Smell the Roses on page 88
Text: "Yesterday"
Oil on canvas, 16" x 20" – 2010
Subject: Color study of a rose
This painting is the result of a color study. I used a simple rose as a subject. The color scheme goes from yellow to orange to red.

Chapter 5

Divine Guidance

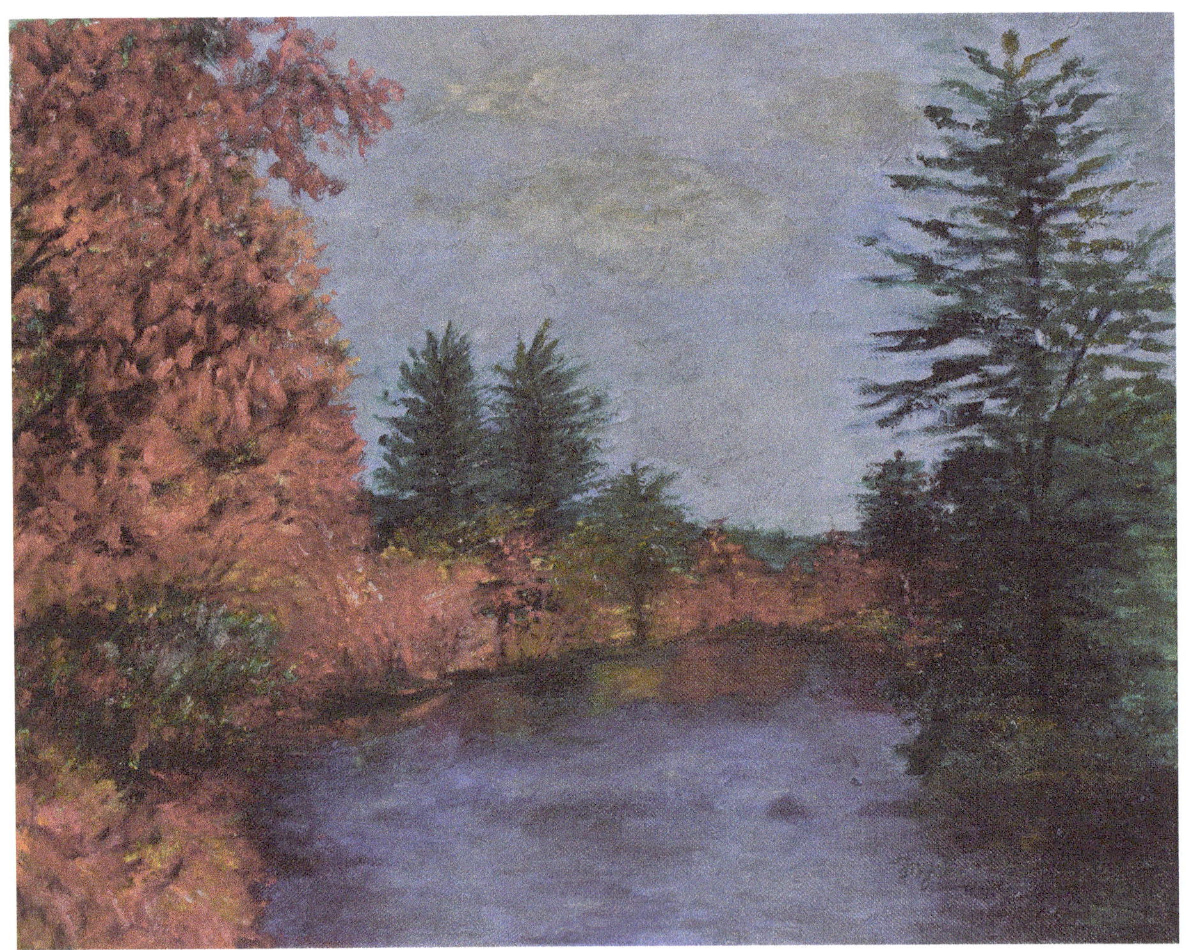

Thank Me

Thank Me for everything that
happens in your life
for everything has its purpose.

You are My messenger from heaven
send to earth to spread My light and
share it with your brothers and sisters.

Rejoice in all circumstances together and
praise the experience of life on earth.

You all are very, very important and
nothing can be done without the other.

Blessed be your wonderful souls and
blessed be your path.

Ingeborg Martinez

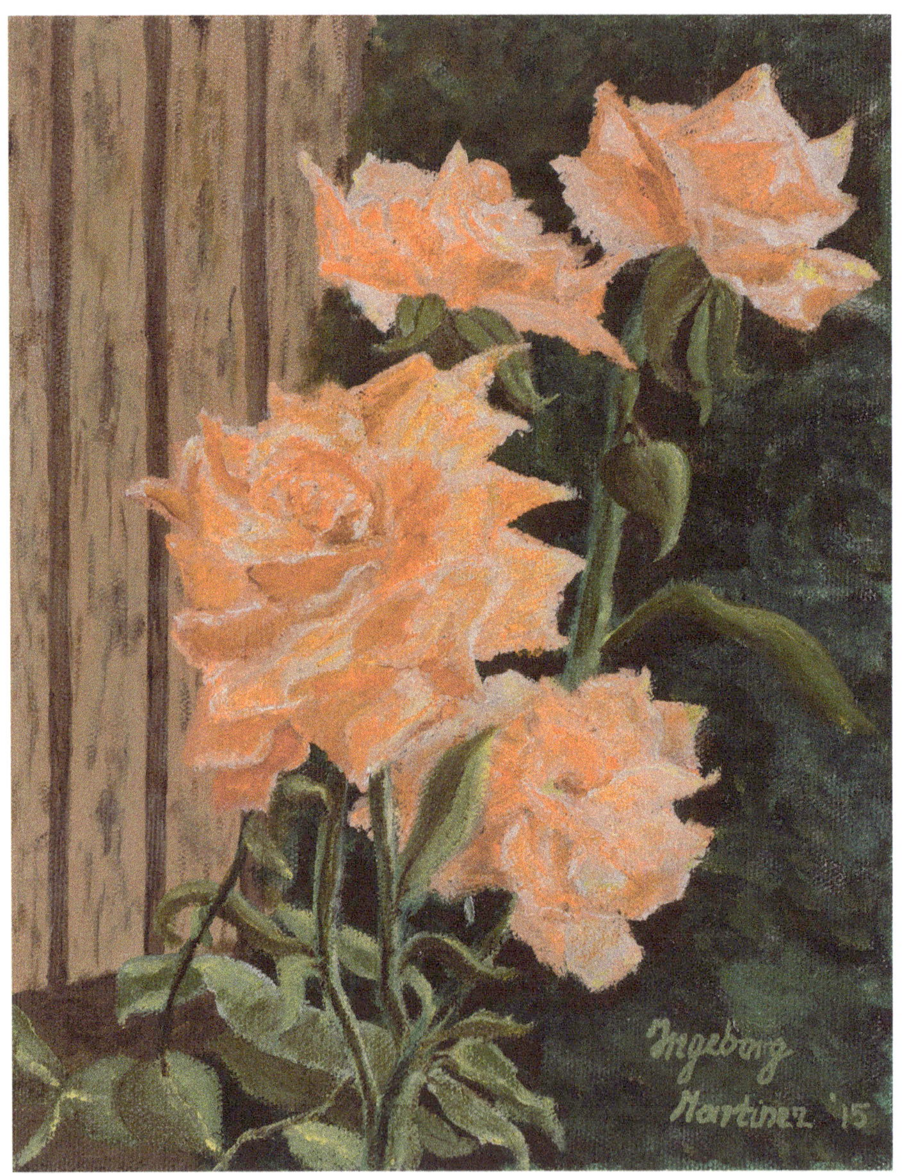

A Grateful Heart

A grateful heart opens up the doors to heaven
letting pour in your wants and desires.

With thankfulness receive my blessings
and let them be multiplied.

The more you receive, the more you can give.
The more you give, the more you will receive.
This applies to everything!

So be careful for what you want in your life.
Positive attracts positive.
Negative attracts negative.

Ask for grateful thoughts and
you will bask in light.

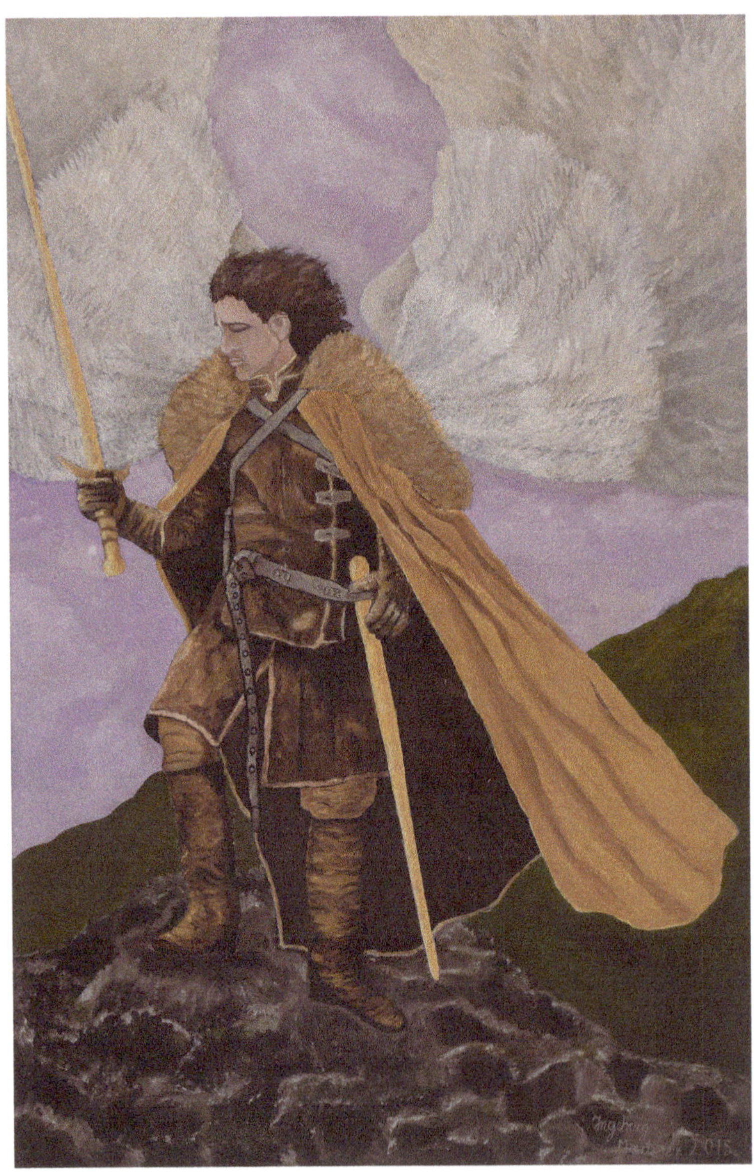

Never Alone

You are never alone!
My guidance is always with you.

Be still and listen to My gentle voice
speaking to you in loving whispers
assuring you every step of your way.

My light shines around you
in warmth and appreciation.

My dear child,
let Me tell you how grateful
I am for your faithful service.

Imagine yourself covered in my loving hands,
protected from all harm and insecurities.

You are my sonship:
Now, Yesterday and Forever!

Ingeborg Martinez

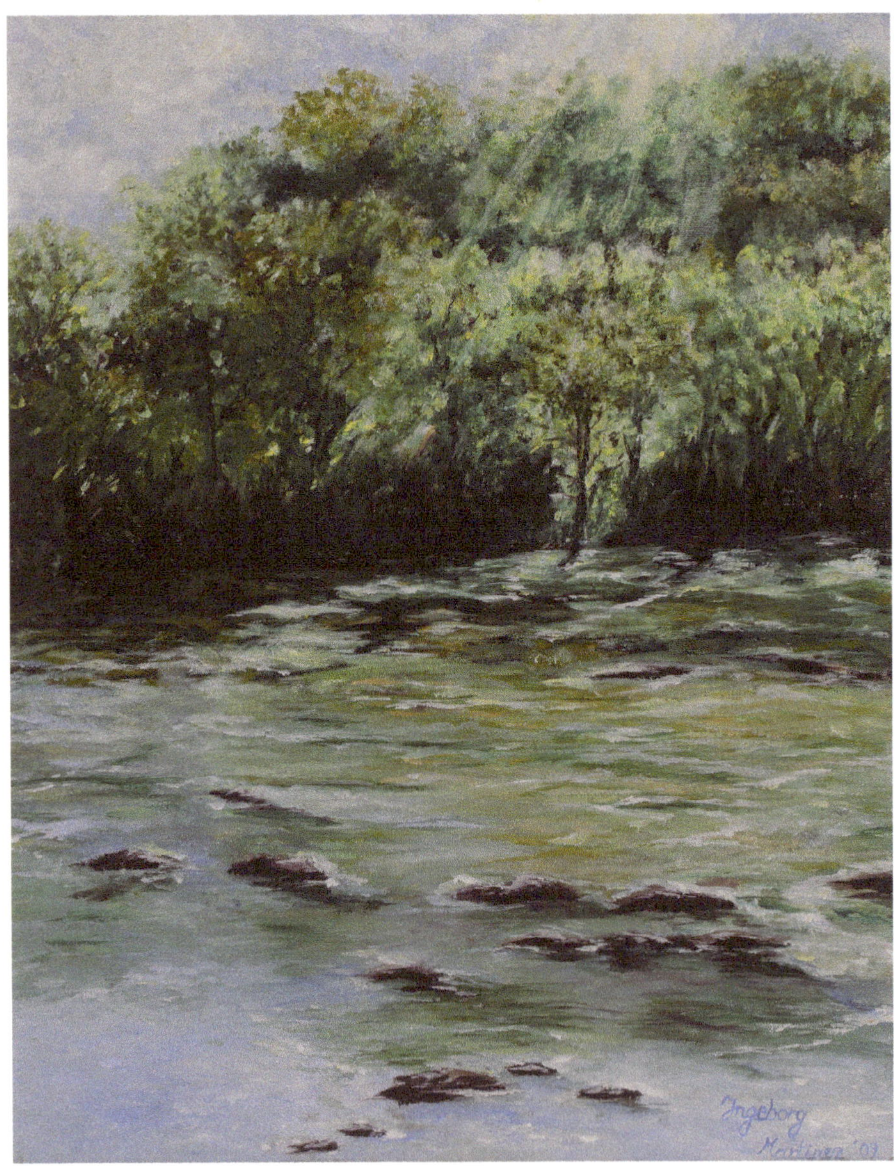

Letting Go

To *Let GO* is one of the hardest lessons to learn.

You have so much love for your attachments and
dreams not knowing that they are not your path.

Taken away, you crumble and shake in
disappointment, wailing and whining.

But there is a silver lining at the horizon:
Everything has a purpose found
in the big and the small.

Here is where faith and trust are needed.

Trust in ME, your Creator!
I know the why and the reason.

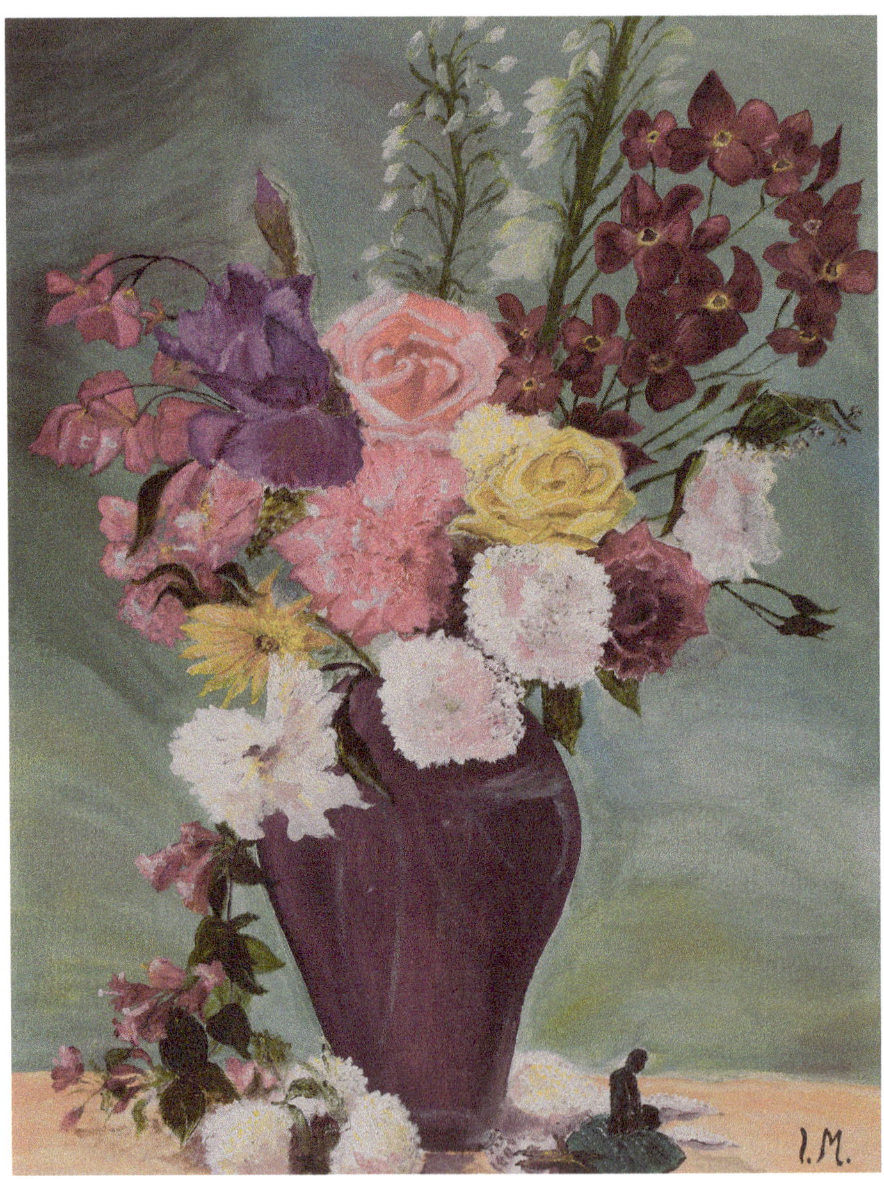

Strong Faith

Never ever let go of faith in ME,
your true GOD!

Spring and Summer bring sunshine,
flowers and dance.

Fall and Winter bring harvest and rest.

I bring life to you throughout
the year.

Never forget,
I AM the *True Source* for everything!

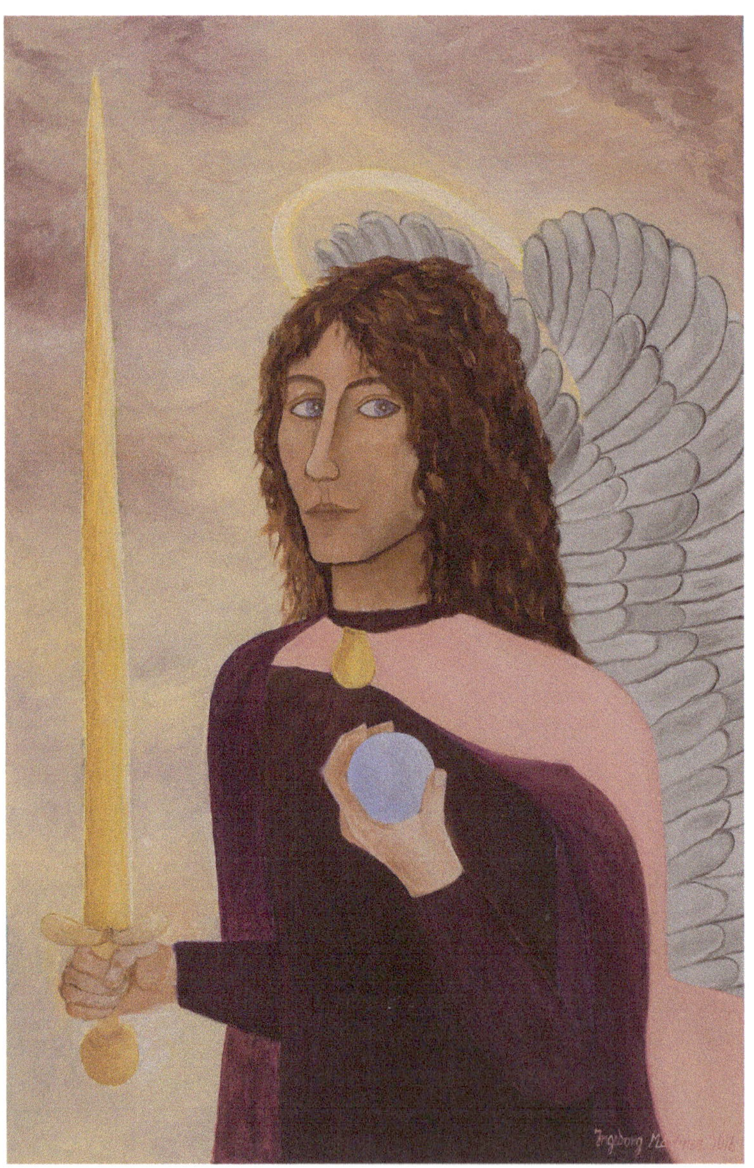

Trust Your Guidance

Always trust the guidance of
your own precious heart.

The mind plays tricks on you.

Nevertheless, your heart, filled
with joy coming from GOD,
is your true and only path.

Mercy showered on all and everything
brings you closer to your TRUE SELF,
bestowing yourself in the process with
everlasting peace and abundance of joy.

Walk with ME, your Creator,
every single path and not one stone
can hurt your wonderful feet!

Ingeborg Martinez

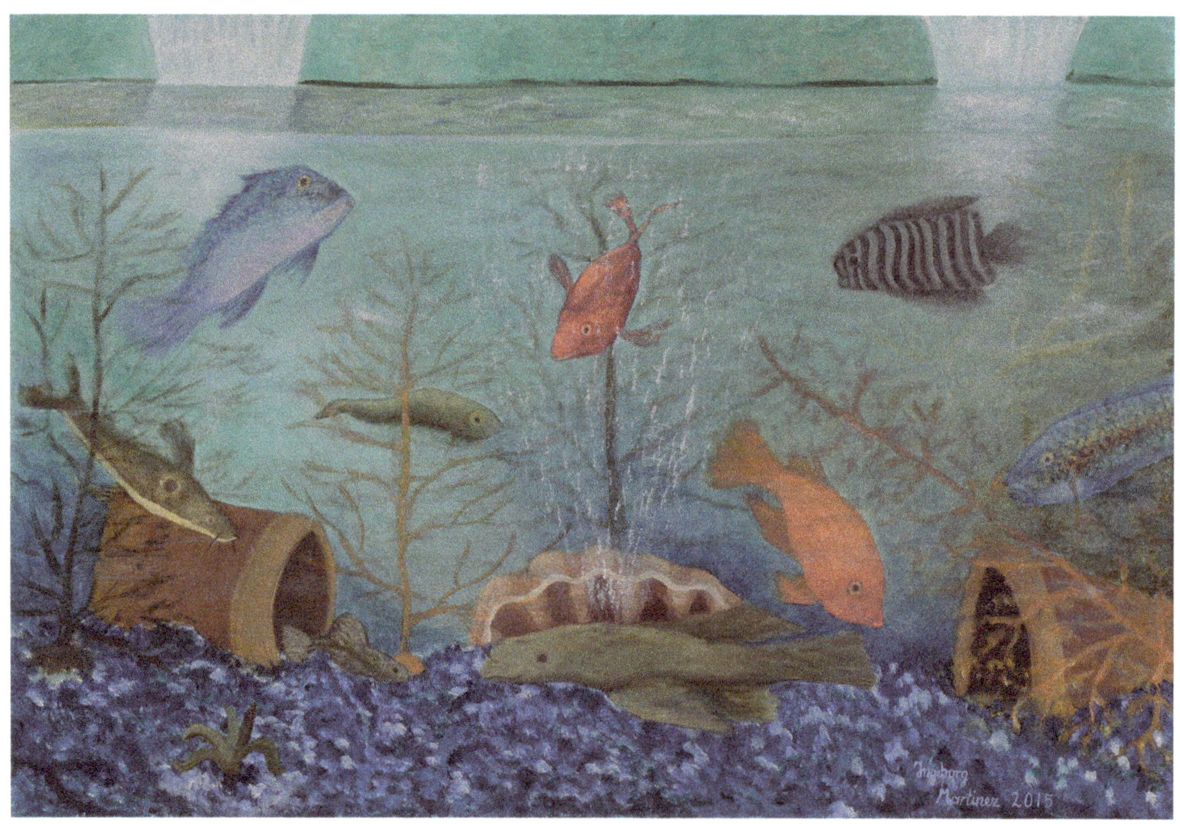

True Trust

Trust is something you do not
really have a grasp of.

First of all, you put your trust into
people, institutions, schools, earthly
teachings, etc. around you, only to be
constantly misled and disappointed.

This behavior has become a habit for you, and
I am telling you the time has come to break it.

Start to listen more closely to your own inner self:
What are its dreams, emotions and desires?

This is the first lesson in building
TRUE TRUST:
Listen to yourself first!

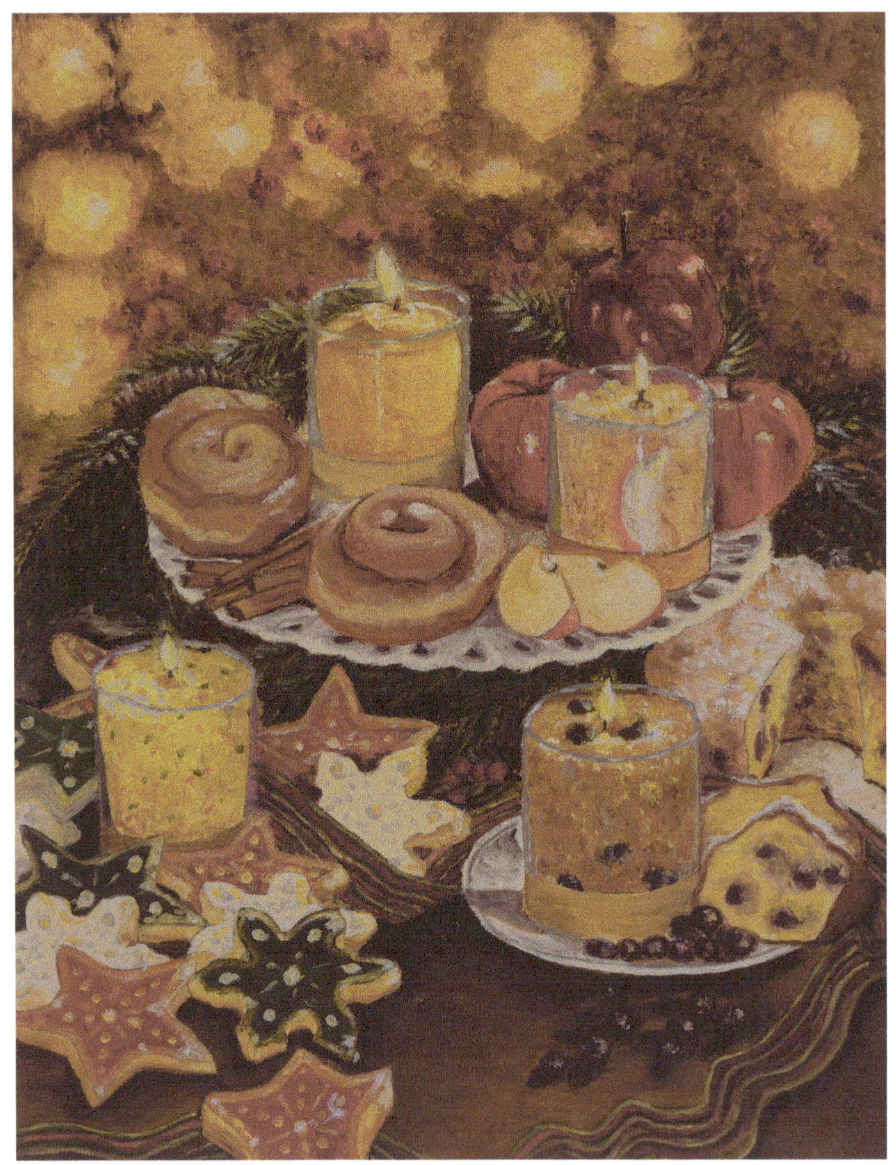

A Christmas Greeting

Never mistrust your inner guidance.

The first hunch is the truth
before the mind and logic jumps in
to try and convince you otherwise.

You are listening more and more
to those inner nudging's.
That's why your life is so peaceful and
harmonious right now.

I am your Spirit Guide and my
task with you is so pleasant.

You and I are in true harmony
and heaven rejoices in our
successful collaboration.

Merry Christmas to you and know
that we are celebrating with you!

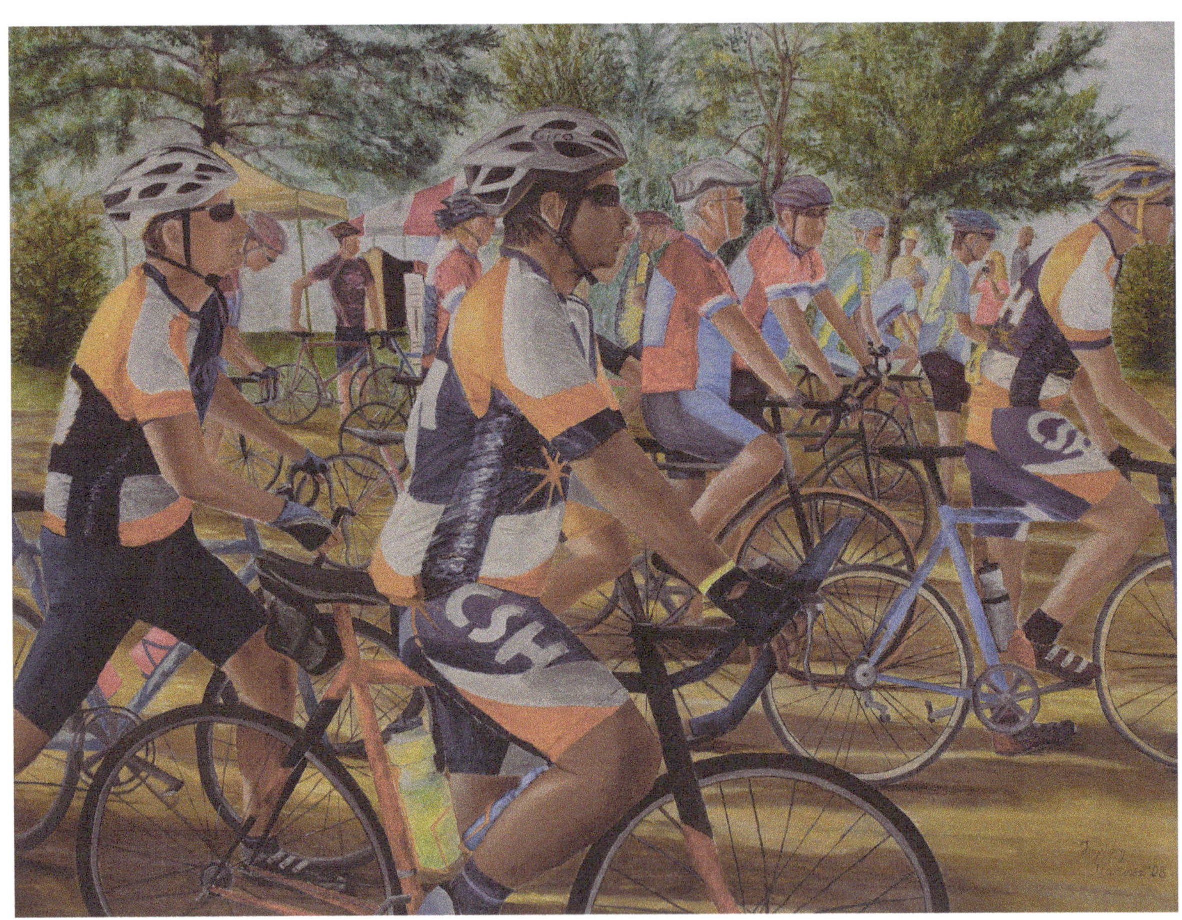

Challenges and Opportunities

Every day brings new challenges into your life.
Every day brings new opportunities
for growth and shining your light.

You are very important in the scheme of life.
Never underestimate the impact
of your presence wherever you are!

You are truly the light of the world.
Let your light shine and make
the world a brighter place.

You are Love:
Go out and show it to the world!

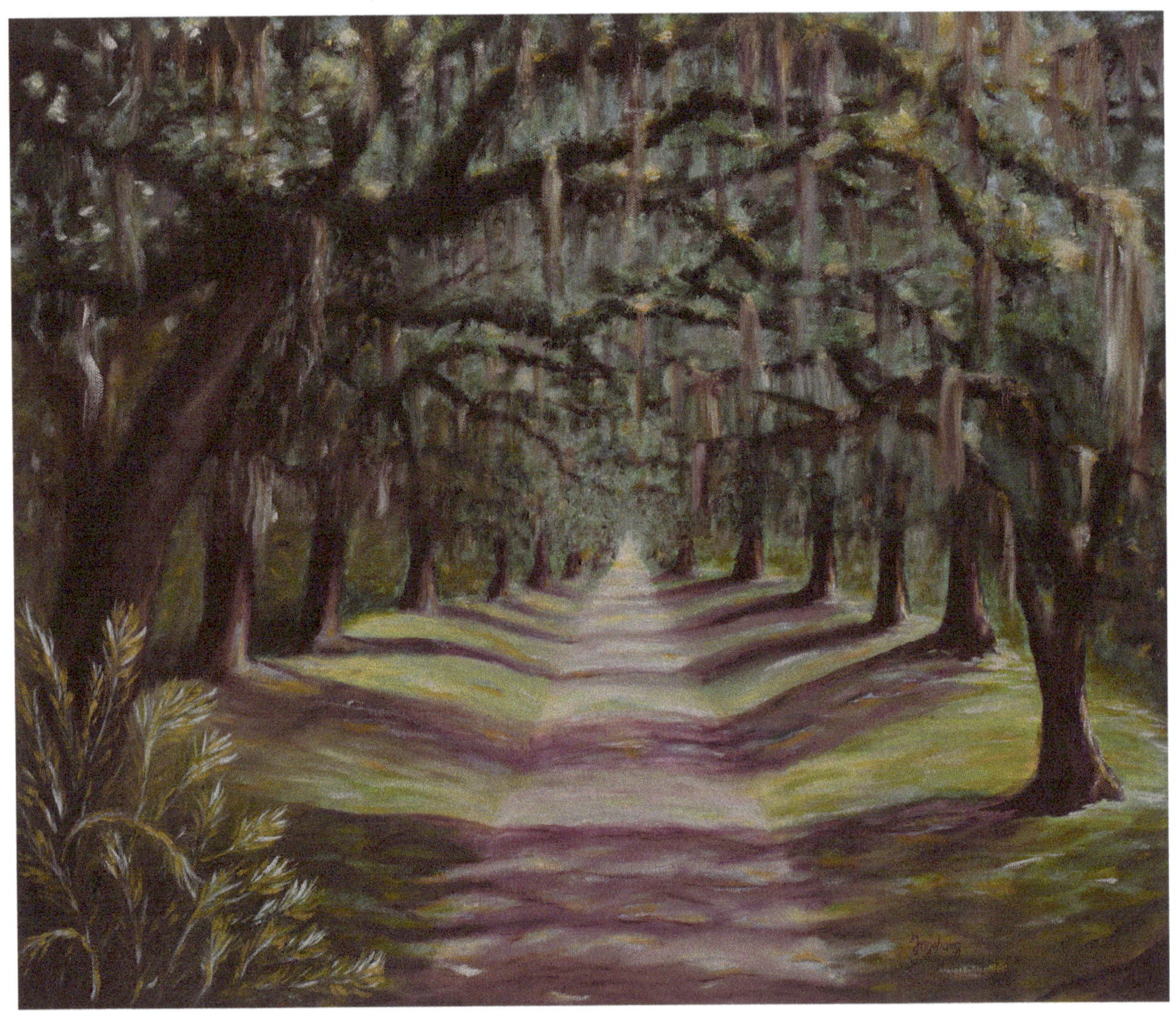

The Right Path

You are on your path.
Heaven gives you all blessings.
In the midst of the storm
you have fought a brave battle;
Winning is the outcome!

Blessings to you and your warm, loving heart.
Blessings on your house and belongings.
Blessings on your loved ones and
those who are truly with you.

We are thoroughly engaged in your daily life and
enjoy every second in your presence.

Blessings on your path because it leads
you back to your true home:
Strengthened, grown and mature.

We are proud of you!!!

Ingeborg Martinez

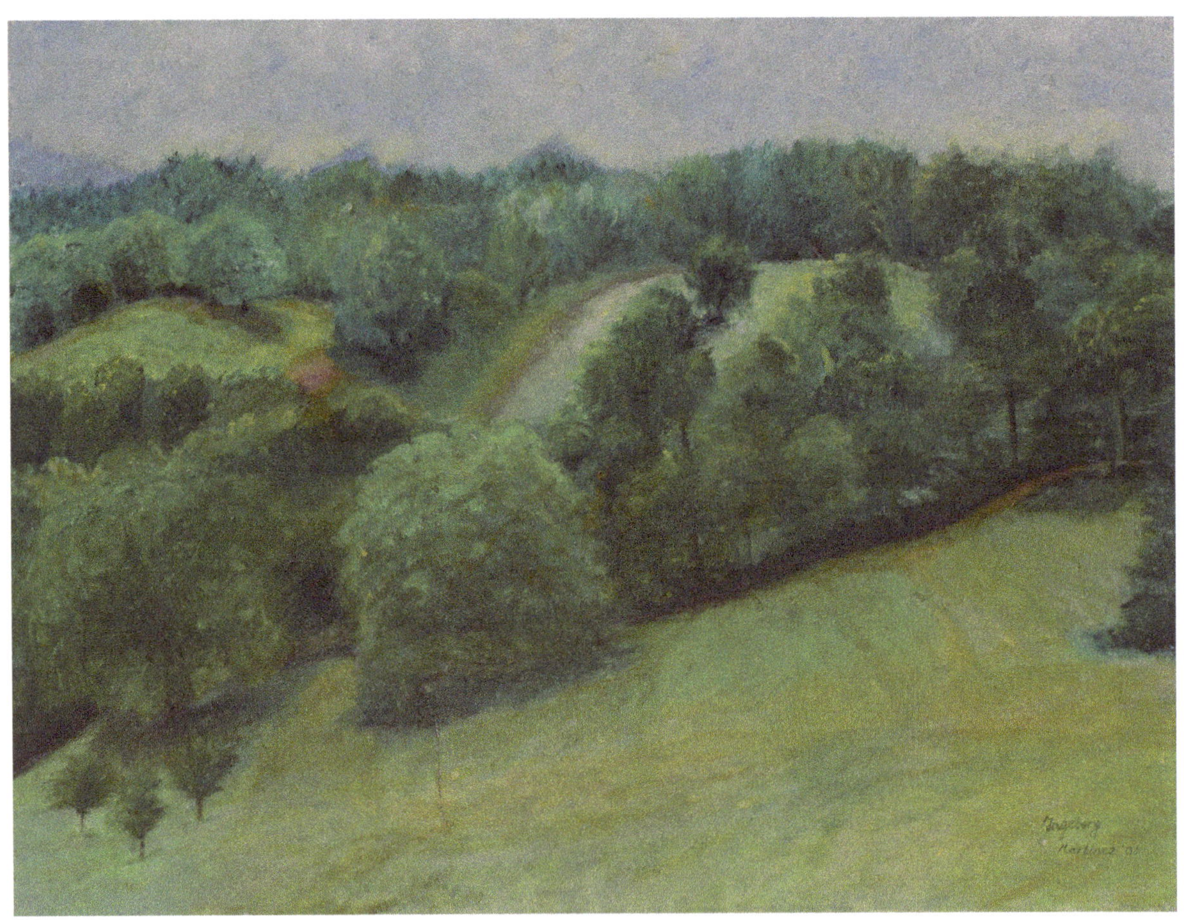

114

Remember ME

Remember ME in your darkest hour
and the light in your heart will
immediately be turned on.

Walk cautiously in My Presence and
be guarded about your thoughts.

Negativity all too easily slips into your
thinking, darkening your path
making it slippery.

The minute you find yourself slipping,
turn your mind right away to Me and
you will again shine and walk in MY Light.

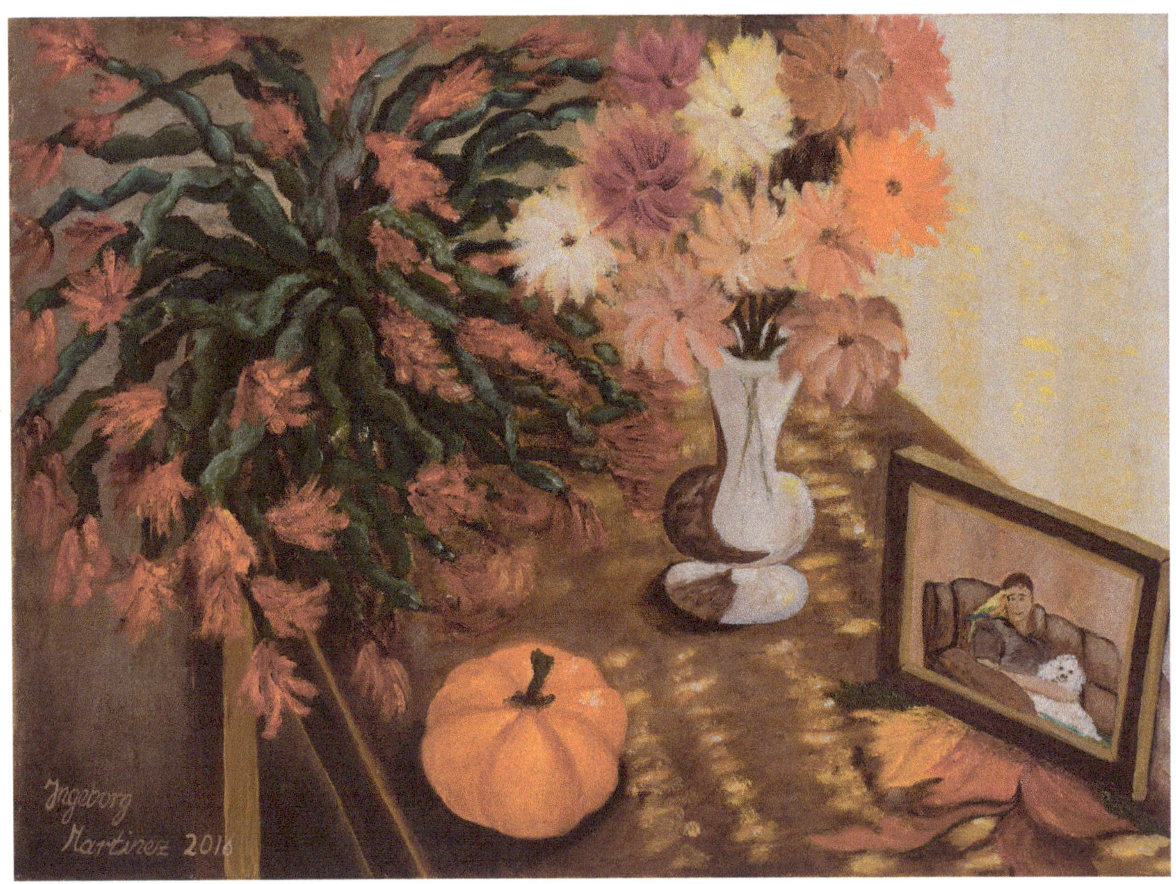

Longing for your Company

I know you can't come into
My Presence every day.

But I want you to know that I,
Your Creator, miss you dearly.

Our conversations are so precious to ME.

I long for your company like a parent being
in the company of his/her beloved child!

Ingeborg Martinez

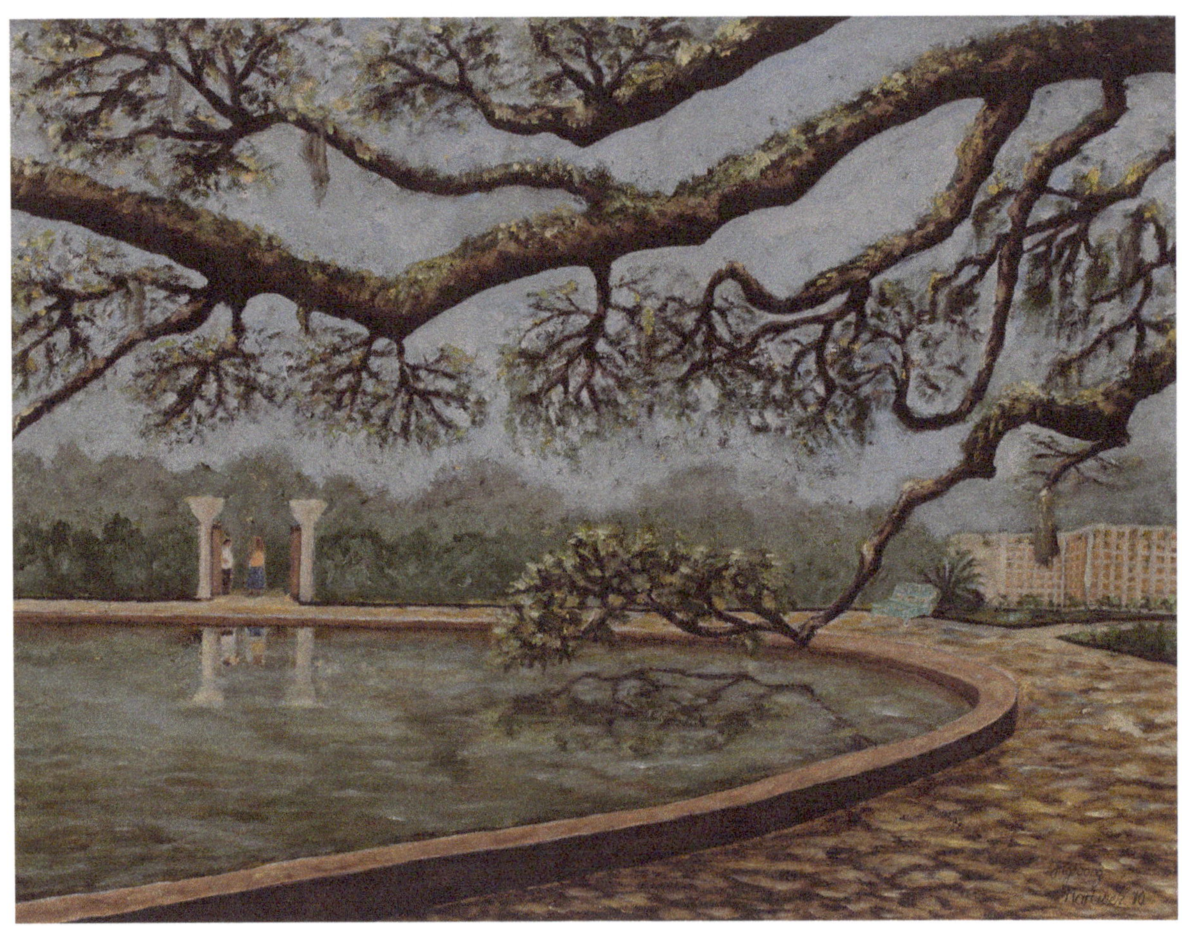

You Need ME

Today you need ME even more than ever.

Your memories are clouded with darkness.
You are in fear of the terrors of your childhood.

In truth, you are my child only!
Your earthly parents just helped you
to enter this world as theirs did for them.

The best way to reconnect with ME,
your TRUE PARENT, is through *forgiveness*.

Everything that happened did so for a reason.
Darkness is needed to see the light.

You are a bright, shining star
sparkling with light.

Only this is the truth!

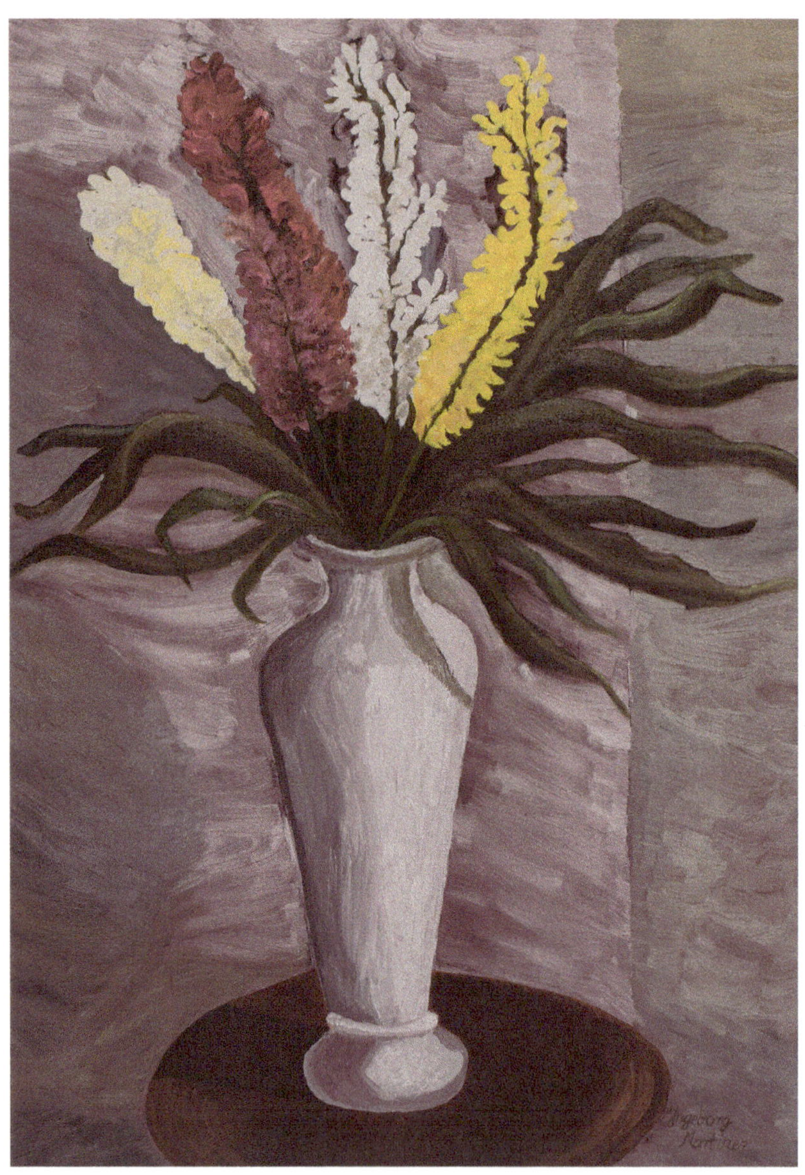

The Journey

You are on an adventurous journey and
the battles are plenty and hard.

I want to compliment you
on your bravery, facing each battle
fiercely and determined.

There is nothing but love and pride
for you in My heart.

What a soldier on mission on earth on My behalf!

I bless you;
I bless this day;
I bless your journey.

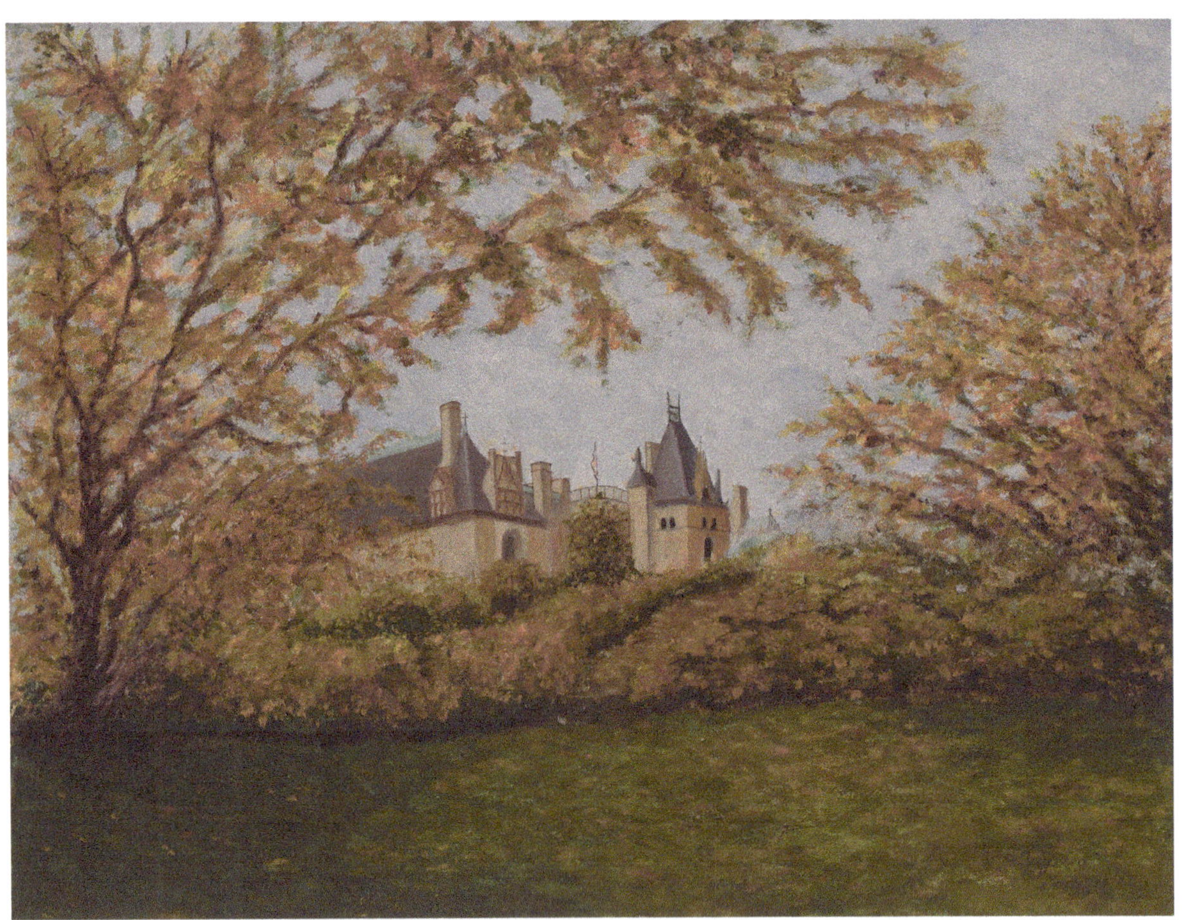

GOD is Speaking

My dearest friend,

I, your GOD, know of your struggles
and deep pain.
I feel it with you and through you.

Thank you for providing ME with this
opportunity to experience pain.
I know how hard this is on you and
I want to let you know that
I am always (all ways) with you.

Everything you are experiencing is planned.
You are exactly at the place where
you are supposed to be.

Nothing is in disorder even though
it appears to you that way.

Let ME tell you one thing that you
need to remember always (all ways):
I love you dearly and I am
with you without ceasing!

Notes

Autumn Red on page 94
Text: "Thank me"
Oil on canvas, 18"x 14" – 2006
Subject: Trees at a lake
Another attempt of my earlier impressionistic paintings. The vibrant autumn colors invited to play with the paint and form a landscape out of it.

The Four Graces on page 96
Text: "A Grateful Heart"
Oil on canvas, 8" x 10" – 2015
Subject: Rose bush
The first-year bloom of a freshly planted rose bush in front of my house. Delighted to right away have such beautiful roses, I needed to memorialize them in a simple painting.

Sirius on page 98
Text: "Never Alone"
Oil on canvas, 24" x 36" – 2015
Subject: My guardian angel
It has been a long-held desire of mine to show my guardian angel on canvas. This is how I picture him: fully prepared to defend me from all harm and negativity.

Beam of Light on page 100
Text: "Letting Go"
Oil on canvas, 16" x 20" – 2009
Subject: French Broad River, North Carolina
My son, Dominic, attended a so-called *time trial* with his race bicycle which was held close to the French Broad River in the mountains of North Carolina. It was a beautiful day at the end of summer and the photos showed up with crisp and clear colors.
In one of them there was a beam of light coming through the trees, reflecting on the water of the river. This is the painted result.

Beauty in Flowers – II on page 102
Text: "Strong Faith"
Oil on canvas, 22" x 28" – 2002
Subject: Variety of flowers in clear vase
Still being in the early stages of painting, I wanted to paint a twin to *Beauty in Flowers – I* attempting to put the floweres in a clear vase. They are a mixture of fantasy and reality.

The Protector on page 104
Text: "Trust Your Guidance"
Oil on canvas, 24" x 36" – 2004
Subject: Archangel Michael
My first attempt at painting an angel. I chose Archangel Michael because I belong to *The Order of Archangel Michael* fulfilling my part here on earth under his protection.

Ingeborg Martinez

Something Fishy on page 106
Text: "True Trust"
Oil on canvas, 36" x 24" – 2015
Subject: South American Cichlids in home aquarium
As my son moved out of the house starting his own life, he left an inheritance behind: a fish tank in his room full of a wide variety of fish.
In the beginning, I was totally overwhelmed taking care of them. It didn't take long and I fell in love with the critters and after three years, I am well acquainted with being a "fish Mommy."
Now I know that each fish has its own personality and that there is a certain kind of structure in the fish community. Some are aggressive and have to be kept away from the calm ones by a divider.
My love also expressed itself in giving each fish its own name:
From left to right, top to bottom:
Tiger Eye (cat fish); Carpy senior (cichlid); Sharpy (knife fish); Slushy (Japanese algae eater); Goldilocks (cichlid); Slurpy (algae eater); Charger (cichlid); Blacky (cichlid); Carpy Junior (cichlid).

Christmas Goodies on page 108
Text: "A Christmas Greeting"
Oil on canvas, 11" x 14" – 2010
Subject: Christmas Table
Every year, I paint a Christmas motif to make my own Christmas cards, sending them to family and friends around the world. In this scenery, I wanted to explore the holiday colors, inducing the tastes and smells of the season.

Charity Ride on page 110
Text: "Challenges and Opportunities"
Oil on canvas, 40" x 30" – 2008
Subject: MS 150 Ride, New Bern, North Carolina
The bicycle rider in the front is my son, Dominic, at the age of 16 years. He was in the beginning of his junior bicycle racing activities and eager to attend the *MS150 Charity Ride* held in New Bern, North Carolina. We spent a marvelous weekend there. We entertained ourselves by visiting the town, eating and drinking. Dominic rode his bicycle for two days, 100 miles each day.

Mystery Garden on page 112
Text: "The Right Path"
Oil on canvas, 20" x 24" – 2009
Subject: Brookgreen Gardens, South Carolina
A marvelous path opened before us while leisurely walking through Brookgreen Gardens. What a beautiful painting it turned into, full of mystery and promises.

Lushes Green on page 114
Text: "Remember ME"
Oil on canvas, 24" x 18" – 2006
Subject: Biltmore Estate, Asheville, North Carolina
This view is the backyard of Biltmore Estate, Asheville, North Carolina. Included in the tour through the main house is a walk onto the back patio. Of course, the patio is huge and the view is gorgeous. I took several photos and while I was looking at them, an idea formed in my mind: use only green color to form the backyard. Just the sky has a light blue, the rest is all formed out of different shades of green, mixed with ocher and Vandyke brown.

Ingeborg Martinez

Christmas Cactus in Fall on page 116
Text: "Longing for your Company"
Oil on canvas, 16" x 22" – 2016
Subject: Side table with flowers and objects
It was fall 2014 and everything was decorated in autumn and Halloween colors. On my side table near the window, I had mums and a Christmas cactus that was supposed to bloom in December. But instead I had an early bloomer, mixed with my fall decoration.
The photo that I took looked so gorgeous, I just had to paint the composition on canvas.

Touching Grace on page 118
Text: "You Need ME"
Oil on canvas, 24" x 18" – 2010
Subject: Brookgreen Gardens, South Carolina
Another calming lake in Brookgreen Gardens. The branches of this oak tree covered in moss almost touched the water. What an exciting composition to bring on canvas!

The White Vase on page 120
Text: "The Journey"
Oil on canvas, 20" x 28" – 1996
Subject: Vase and flowers on table
This is the fourth painting after I started to paint. The first three were small ones just to practice. Here I was already a bit bolder and chose a larger canvas and more demanding composition.

Biltmore Estate Fall on page 122
Text: "GOD is Speaking"
Oil on canvas, 24" x 18" – 2008
Subject: Biltmore Estate, Asheville, North Carolina
The fourth of my series of Biltmore Estate paintings. This is set in the fall season.

About the Author

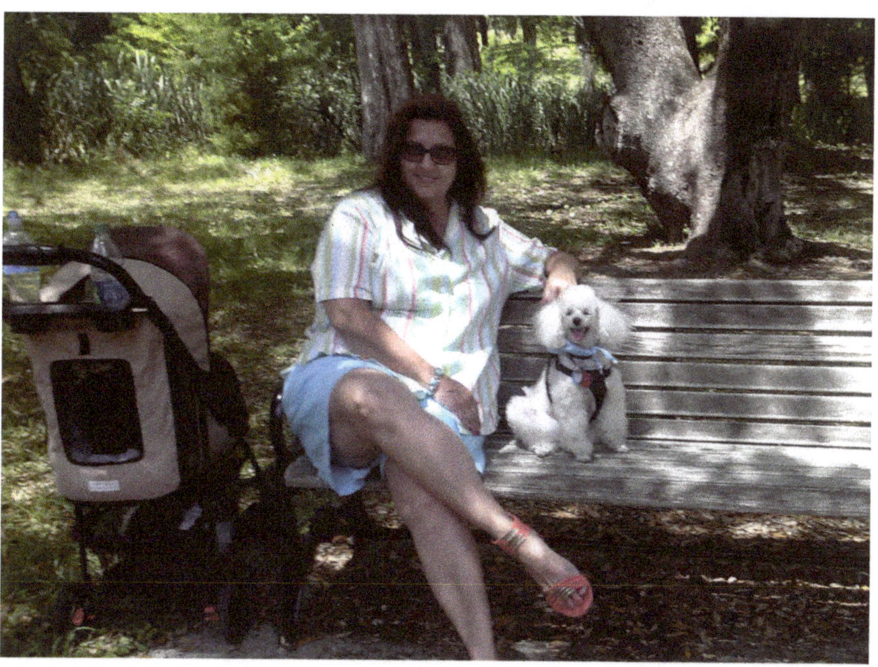

Born and raised in Stuttgart, Germany, I immigrated to the USA with my American husband and two small children in December 1998. Life in Germany consisted of being educated academically through school and spiritually in the Roman Catholic Church. From 1970 to 1998, I worked for Daimler-Benz in Stuttgart as an executive secretary. After achieving a bachelor's degree in business, I held an interesting position in the Controlling and Budgeting Department for trucks.

Ingeborg Martinez

My second marriage was blessed with two children whom we adopted from Romania. For several years, I was a mom who worked part time, either at night or during school hours. Coming to the USA, I decided to be only a home maker. While my children were at school, I had time to acclimate myself to the new surroundings: learning the English language, attending Lifelong Education at North Carolina State University, and meeting many wonderful people in my pursuit of my spiritual life.

Health issues interrupted my goal of studying psychology at North Carolina State University and I started to dig even deeper into the world of metaphysics. At the same time, I attended the Pullen Arts Center on a regular basis to improve my artistic talent.

So far I have created about one hundred paintings and this is my first book. Receiving spiritual messages through left-hand writing, I felt compelled to combine paintings and text and publish them in book form. My second marriage suddenly ended after twenty-seven years. I am living with my 14-year-old toy poodle, "Snowball," in Raleigh and devote most of my time to painting and receiving messages from the spirit world.

Email address: ingeborgmartinez2@gmail.com

Website: www.Ingasart.com

Facebook: https://www.facebook.com/ingeborg.martinez

Instagram https://www.instagram.com/ingeborgmartinez/

My companies name: Inga's Art from the Heart, Inc.

www.ingramcontent.com/pod-product-compliance
Lightning Source LLC
Chambersburg PA
CBHW041029050726

47599CB00018B/1905